for the Family

Marguerite Patten

Hamlyn
London · New York · Sydney · Toronto

Published by
The Hamlyn Publishing Group Limited
London · New York · Sydney · Toronto
Hamlyn House, Feltham, Middlesex, England

ISBN 0 600 30203 2
Printed in England by Sir Joseph Causton and Sons Limited
Line drawings by John Scott Martin

Contents

Useful facts and figures 4
Introduction 6

Baking with yeast 8-25
White bread – tin loaf 8
Cob loaf 10
Lardy cake 12
Swedish tea ring 14
Sally Lunns 16
Fruit bannock 18
Hot cross buns 20
Chelsea buns 22
Croissants 24

Scones, buns and teabreads 26-57
Devonshire cream scones and
Cream cheese scones 26
Cheese and bacon scones 28
Cheese scone round 30
Hot apple muffins 32
American ring doughnuts 34
Oaties 36
Rock buns 38
Raisin bread 40
Wholemeal date loaf 42
Soda bread 44
Honey squares 46
Cream buns 48
Sticky gingerbread 50
Blueberry bread 52
Glazed cherry bread 54
Canadian apple nut bread 56

Family cakes 58-93
American apple cake 58
Sultana loaf 60
Speedy orange cake 62
Spiced honey cake 64
Honey, date and walnut cake
and Honey loaf 66
Sand cake 68
Cherry cake 70
Apple cake 72
Family fruit cake 74
Economical light fruit cake 76
Chocolate walnut cake 78
Surprise cake 80
Victoria sandwich 82
Sponge cake 84
Swiss roll 86
Gugelhupf 88
Apfelstrudel 90
Streusel torte 92

Gâteaux 94-115
Rich chocolate cake 94
Moist chocolate sandwich 96
Devil's food cake 98
Strawberry shortcake 100
Coffee carnival gâteau 102
Chocolate bar gâteau 104
West Indian gâteau 106
Marshmallow gâteau 108
Cherry and almond cake 110
Honey almond dessert cake 112
Festive cream gâteau 114

Special-occasion cakes 116-119
Mother's day cake 116
Simnel cake 118

Small cakes and biscuits 120-127
Coffee frosted brownies 120
Ginger prune crunch 122
Chocolate and walnut cookies 124
Brandy snaps 126

Acknowledgements 128

Useful facts and figures

Note on metrication

In this book quantities are given in both Imperial and metric measures. Exact conversion from Imperial to metric does not always give very convenient working quantities so for greater convenience and ease of working we have taken an equivalent of 25 grammes/millilitres to the ounce/fluid ounce. 1 oz. is exactly 28·35 g. and ¼ pint (5 fl. oz.) is 142 ml., so you will see that by using the unit of 25 you will get a slightly smaller result than the Imperial measures would give.

Occasionally, for example in a basic recipe such as a Victoria sandwich made with 4 oz. flour, butter and sugar and 2 eggs, we have rounded the conversion up to give a more generous result. For larger amounts where the exact conversion is not critical, for instance in soups or stews, we have used kilogrammes and fractions (1 kg. equals 2·2 lb.) and litres and fractions (1 litre equals 1·76 pints). All recipes have been individually converted so that each recipe preserves the correct proportions.

Oven temperatures

The following chart gives the Celsius (Centigrade) equivalents recommended by the Electricity Council.

Description	Fahrenheit	Celsius	Gas Mark
Very cool	225	110	¼
	250	130	½
Cool	275	140	1
	300	150	2
Moderate	325	170	3
	350	180	4
Moderately hot	375	190	5
	400	200	6
Hot	425	220	7
	450	230	8
Very hot	475	240	9

Introduction

I know, from meeting so many women when I am giving demonstrations throughout the country, that there is still a great interest in home baking. I think that nothing is more rewarding than a delicious home-made cake or a loaf of crusty bread coming fresh from the oven.

Many people think that bread making is difficult. Baking breads and buns with yeast is really simple and makes a most relaxing hobby, and I am sure that as you gain experience you will really enjoy handling the dough. More and more people today are interested in bread making especially as it is possible to freeze extra bread and buns to enjoy another day!

Many countries have one or two recipes which are particular favourites and in this book I have included a few of these. American ring doughnuts, Croissants, Canadian apple bread, Gugelhupf, Apfelstrudel and West Indian gâteau are to be found among our own traditional favourites such as Devonshire cream scones, Sticky gingerbread and Parkin.

A cake packed away in a tin is always useful for unexpected guests and children still like mother's baking best! I hope this colourful book will provide you with a few more family favourites to add to your baking repertoire.

Marguerite Patten

White bread – tin loaf

Cooking time: 30–40 minutes
Preparation time: 20 minutes plus time for dough to prove
Main cooking utensil: 1-lb. ($\frac{1}{2}$-kg.) loaf tin
Oven temperature: very hot (450–475°F., 230–240°C., Gas Mark 8–9)
Oven position: centre
Makes: 1 small loaf

Imperial	**Metric**
Yeast liquid:	*Yeast liquid:*
1 teaspoon sugar	1 teaspoon sugar
½ pint warm water	250 ml. warm water
½ oz. fresh yeast or 1 level dessertspoon dried yeast	15 g. fresh yeast or 1 level dessertspoon dried yeast
Dry ingredients:	*Dry ingredients:*
½ oz. lard or margarine	15 g. lard or margarine
1 lb. flour	400 g. flour
1–2 level teaspoons salt	1–2 level teaspoons salt

1. Dissolve the sugar in the warm water. With fresh yeast add liquid and use immediately, or see next recipe. With dried yeast sprinkle on top of liquid – leave for 10 minutes or until mixture becomes frothy – known as 'letting the sponge break through' or 'sponging'.
2. Rub the lard into flour and salt, sieved into a warm bowl. (All yeast utensils need to be warm.)
3. Add yeast liquid, knead well.
4. Cover bowl with a cloth or put dough into a greased, large polythene bag.
5. Allow to rise until double its size; this takes about 45–60 minutes in a warm place – 2 hours in a cool room. This is known as 'proving'.
6. Re-knead dough (called 'knocking back'); continue kneading until dough springs back when pressed with a floured finger.
7. To shape loaf press to oblong, fold in three and put in a greased warm tin.
8. Prove again until risen to the top of the tin.
9. Bake for time and at temperature given; reduce heat if over-browning.

To test: Knock bottom of loaf – it should sound hollow.
Note: The liquid in yeast cooking should not exceed 100°F. (38°C.). Preferably use strong flour – a little more may be needed as makes of flour vary in the amount of liquid they absorb.

Cob loaf

Cooking time: 30–40 minutes
Preparation time: 20 minutes plus time for dough to prove
Main cooking utensil: flat baking sheet
Oven temperature: very hot (450–475°F., 230–240°C., Gas Mark 8–9)
Oven position: centre
Makes: 1 small loaf

Imperial	**Metric**
Yeast liquid:	*Yeast liquid:*
1 teaspoon sugar	1 teaspoon sugar
$\frac{1}{2}$ pint warm water	250 ml. warm water
$\frac{1}{2}$ oz. fresh yeast or 1 level dessertspoon dried yeast	15 g. fresh yeast or 1 level dessertspoon dried yeast
Dry ingredients:	*Dry ingredients:*
$\frac{1}{2}$ oz. lard or margarine	15 g. lard or margarine
1 lb. flour	400 g. flour
1–2 level teaspoons salt	1–2 level teaspoons salt
Coating:	*Coating:*
little extra flour	little extra flour

1. Prepare the yeast liquid as in preceding recipe or cream the yeast and sugar, add the warm liquid, sprinkle the top with flour and leave in a warm place until the sponge breaks through.
2. Continue as page 9, stages 2 to 6.
3. To shape the cob loaf, mould dough into a round ball, flatten slightly and cut top of loaf with a sharp knife.
4. Dredge with a little extra flour, put on to a lightly floured tray to prove. Cover with greased polythene if wished and leave till double in size.
5. Bake for time and at temperature given.
6. Test as on page 9. Store in an airtight tin or bread bin.

Note: For explanation of yeast cookery terms see page 9. The liquid in yeast cooking should not exceed 100°F. (38°C.). It is best to use strong flour in bread making.

Variations

Cottage loaf: Divide dough into one large and one small portion. Roll in balls; press small ball on top of large, make cut on top. Bake as above.

Brown bread: Use half white and half wholemeal flour, plus a little extra liquid.

Wholemeal bread: Use all stone-ground flour plus extra liquid to give a soft dough. This takes longer to prove and bake.

Lardy cake

Cooking time: approximately 45 minutes
Preparation time: 25 minutes plus 15 minutes at stage 1, 1–1½ hours first proving, 30–40 minutes second proving
Main cooking utensil: 12- by 7-inch (30- by 18-cm.) tin or 8-inch (20-cm.) tin or baking sheet
Oven temperature: hot (400–425°F., 200–220°C., Gas Mark 6–7), reducing after 20 minutes if necessary
Makes: 14 slices

Imperial	**Metric**
Bread dough:	*Bread dough:*
$\frac{1}{2}$ oz. fresh yeast or 2 level teaspoons dried yeast	15 g. fresh yeast or 2 level teaspoons dried yeast
1 teaspoon sugar	1 teaspoon sugar
about $\frac{1}{2}$ pint tepid water	about 250 ml. tepid water
1 lb. plain flour	400 g. plain flour
$\frac{1}{2}$ teaspoon salt	$\frac{1}{2}$ teaspoon salt
Filling:	*Filling:*
4 oz. lard	100 g. lard
4 oz. sugar	100 g. sugar
4 oz. currants	100 g. currants
a little spice	a little spice
Glaze:	*Glaze:*
2 tablespoons sugar mixed with 2 tablespoons water	2 tablespoons sugar mixed with 2 tablespoons water

1. Cream yeast with sugar, add the tepid water and a little flour; or blend dried yeast with sugar and a little liquid, stand until softened, cream, add rest of liquid and a sprinkling of flour.
2. Put in a warm place until covered with bubbles, add to the sieved flour and salt.
3. Knead thoroughly, cover with a tea-towel or polythene and allow to prove, i.e., rise until double original size.
4. Knead again until smooth, roll out on a floured board to a neat oblong.
5. Put half the lard in small pieces over two thirds of the dough.
6. Sprinkle with half the sugar, fruit and spice, then fold in three, bringing the uncovered piece of dough over first.
7. Give a half turn, repeat 5 and 6.
8. Turn again, roll to a neat oblong, fold, turn and re-roll.
9. Fold once more then roll out to fit warmed tin; score the top.
10. Cover and allow to prove until well risen. Bake in the centre of the oven until golden brown, then remove from tin and test. Knock base, cake should sound hollow. Glaze at once.

Swedish tea ring

Cooking time: 30–35 minutes
Preparation time: 45 minutes plus time for dough to prove
Main cooking utensil: flat baking tray or sheet
Oven temperature: moderate (350–375°F., 180–190°C., Gas Mark 4–5)
Oven position: centre
Serves: 12

Imperial	Metric
$\frac{1}{2}$ oz. fresh yeast or 1 teaspoon dried yeast	15 g. fresh yeast or 1 teaspoon dried yeast
$\frac{1}{2}$ teaspoon sugar	$\frac{1}{2}$ teaspoon sugar
6 tablespoons warm milk	6 tablespoons warm milk
8 oz. plain flour	200 g. plain flour
pinch salt	pinch salt
1 egg	1 egg
1 tablespoon oil	1 tablespoon oil
Filling:	*Filling:*
1 oz. butter	25 g. butter
4 oz. brown sugar	100 g. brown sugar
1–2 teaspoons cinnamon	1–2 teaspoons cinnamon
Decoration:	*Decoration:*
6 oz. icing sugar	150 g. icing sugar
1 tablespoon warm water	1 tablespoon warm water
1 oz. glacé cherries	25 g. glacé cherries
1–2 oz. nuts	25–50 g. nuts

1. If using fresh yeast cream with the sugar, add warm milk; sprinkle dried yeast on to the sugar and milk.
2. Add 2 oz. (50 g.) of the flour, beat well, put into a warm place for 20 minutes until the sponge breaks through.
3. Sieve rest of the flour and salt, add yeast liquid, beaten egg and oil.
4. Knead well, then cover and allow to prove for about 1 hour until double original size.
5. Knock back, knead again until smooth then roll out to an oblong.
6. Brush with the melted butter, sprinkle with the brown sugar and cinnamon.
7. Roll up tightly and seal ends together.
8. Lift on to a greased warm baking tray, and make cuts 1 inch ($2\frac{1}{2}$ cm.) apart and $\frac{1}{2}$ inch (1 cm.) from centre.
9. Allow to prove for 20–30 minutes until well risen.
10. Bake for time and temperature given until firm to the touch.
11. When cold, cover with icing made by blending sieved icing sugar and water. Top with chopped cherries and nuts. Serve for tea or with coffee.

Sally Lunns

Cooking time: 20 minutes
Preparation time: 25 minutes plus time for dough to prove
Main cooking utensils: small cake tins
Oven temperature: moderate (375°F., 190°C., Gas Mark 5)
Oven position: centre
Serves: 12

Imperial	Metric
1 oz. margarine or fat	25 g. margarine or fat
$\frac{1}{4}$ pint milk	125 ml. milk
$\frac{1}{2}$ oz. yeast	15 g. yeast
1 teaspoon sugar	1 teaspoon sugar
12 oz. flour	300 g. flour
good pinch salt	good pinch salt
2 oz. sugar	50 g. sugar
1 egg	1 egg
Glaze:	*Glaze:*
little melted fat	little melted fat

1. Melt the fat, add the milk, warm to blood heat.
2. Cream the yeast with the teaspoon of sugar.
3. Mix yeast with the milk and fat.
4. Mix the flour, salt and 2 oz. (50 g.) sugar, then add yeast liquid, beaten egg, and beat to a very light dough.
5. Divide into four pieces and knead each.
6. Put into the greased and floured cake tins, prick the tops lightly, and leave to rise to the tops of the tins.
7. Bake for time and at temperature given until firm to the touch.
8. Brush tops with melted fat.

Note: When baking always check oven temperature with that recommended in your cooker instruction card or book.

Variation

Apple Sally Lunns: Use double quantities margarine, yeast, sugar, flour, eggs, but no more milk. Add 4–6 oz. (100–150 g.) raisins and a good $\frac{1}{4}$ pint (150 ml.) apple sauce with the beaten eggs. Make into one round to fit an 8- to 9-inch (20- to 23-cm.) ring tin. Prove for 25–30 minutes. Bake for approximately 45–55 minutes. Mix 6 oz. (150 g.) sieved icing sugar with the juice of 1 lemon and water to give a coating consistency. Glaze bread with this, allow to set. Decorate with apple slices and roughly chopped walnuts (see picture).

Fruit bannock

Cooking time: 15–20 minutes
Preparation time: 25 minutes plus time for dough to prove
Main cooking utensil: flat baking tray or sheet
Oven temperature: moderately hot (400°F., 200°C., Gas Mark 6)
Oven position: towards top
Serves: 8

Imperial	Metric
Yeast batter:	*Yeast batter:*
2 oz. plain flour	50 g. plain flour
1 oz. melted butter or lard	25 g. melted butter or lard
4 tablespoons warm milk	4 tablespoons warm milk
$\frac{1}{4}$ oz. fresh yeast or $\frac{1}{2}$ teaspoon dried yeast	10 g. fresh yeast or $\frac{1}{2}$ teaspoon dried yeast
Additional ingredients:	*Additional ingredients:*
6 oz. plain flour	150 g. plain flour
1 oz. castor sugar	25 g. castor sugar
4 tablespoons warm milk	4 tablespoons warm milk
1 oz. sultanas	25 g. sultanas
1 oz. currants	25 g. currants
$\frac{1}{2}$ oz. chopped candied peel	15 g. chopped candied peel
Glaze:	*Glaze:*
milk	milk

1. Blend batter ingredients together in a mixing bowl and leave for 20–30 minutes until frothy.
2. Add the additional ingredients and mix well.
3. Knead dough thoroughly.
4. Put the dough to prove in a greased polythene bag or covered bowl until double size – about 1 hour.
5. Knead dough until smooth, shape into a ball. Flatten to approximately 8 inches (20 cm.) across and $\frac{1}{2}$ inch (1 cm.) thick.
6. Put on greased and floured tray and slash with sharp knife into eight equal sections.
7. Brush top with milk.
8. Cover with greased polythene if possible. Prove for about 30 minutes.
9. Brush top again with milk.
10. Bake for time and temperature given until firm to the touch. Serve for tea. This bannock is best eaten fresh.

Note: For explanation of yeast cookery terms see page 9.

Variation
Use half white and half stone-ground flour.

Hot cross buns

Cooking time: 15 minutes
Preparation time: 20 minutes plus time for proving
Main cooking utensil: flat baking tins or sheets
Oven temperature: hot (425–450°F., 220–230°C., Gas Mark 7–8)
Oven position: towards top
Makes: 16–18 buns

Imperial	Metric
1 lb. sifted plain flour	400 g. sifted plain flour
½ pint milk or milk and water	250 ml. milk or milk and water
½ oz. yeast	15 g. yeast
pinch salt	pinch salt
2 oz. sugar	50 g. sugar
1 level teaspoon cinnamon	1 level teaspoon cinnamon
1 level teaspoon mixed spice	1 level teaspoon mixed spice
2 oz. butter or margarine	50 g. butter or margarine
3 oz. dried fruit	75 g. dried fruit
1 oz. chopped crystallised peel	25 g. chopped crystallised peel
1 egg	1 egg
Decoration:	*Decoration:*
2 oz. shortcrust pastry	50 g. shortcrust pastry
Glaze:	*Glaze:*
2 oz. sugar	50 g. sugar
2 tablespoons water (or milk)	2 tablespoons water (or milk)

1. Put half the flour into a basin.
2. Heat the milk until tepid, whisk on to yeast, add to flour and leave in a warm place until the top is covered with little bubbles (about 20 minutes). This is called sponging.
3. Sieve rest of flour with dry ingredients, rub in butter, add fruit, bind with egg and yeast liquid.
4. Knead until smooth, cover with a warm cloth or put into a plastic bag and leave to prove for approximately 1–1½ hours until double the original size.
5. Knead once again, divide into portions and shape into neat rounds.
6. Put on to warmed greased baking tins allowing room to rise and spread out.
7. Either mark cross with a knife or make with thin strips of the pastry.
8. Allow to prove for 20 minutes then bake at the temperature given.
9. When the buns come out of the oven, glaze with the sugar and water mixed together.

Chelsea buns

Cooking time: 10–15 minutes
Preparation time: 30 minutes plus time for proving
Main cooking utensil: baking tray or 8- to 9-inch (20- to 23-cm.) square shallow tin
Oven temperature: hot (425–450°F., 220–230°C., Gas Mark 7–8)
Oven position: towards centre
Makes: 9 buns

Imperial

Bun dough:
1 oz. sugar
$\frac{1}{4}$ pint warm milk
$\frac{1}{2}$ oz. fresh yeast or 2 teaspoons dried yeast
8 oz. plain flour
pinch salt

Filling:
1 oz. butter or margarine
1 oz. sugar
2 oz. dried fruit

Glaze:
1 tablespoon hot water
1 tablespoon sugar

Metric

Bun dough:
25 g. sugar
125 ml. warm milk
15 g. fresh yeast or 2 teaspoons dried yeast
200 g. plain flour
pinch salt

Filling:
25 g. butter or margarine
25 g. sugar
50 g. dried fruit

Glaze:
1 tablespoon hot water
1 tablespoon sugar

1. Dissolve 1 teaspoon of the sugar in the warm milk. Stir in the yeast, use at once with fresh yeast or wait 10 minutes with dried yeast until mixture starts to bubble, i.e., the sponge breaks through.
2. Sieve the flour and salt, add rest of sugar and the yeast liquid.
3. Cover with a cloth or put into a polythene bag and allow the mixture to rise, i.e., prove until double its original size (about 50 minutes at room temperature).
4. Knead until smooth, roll out to a neat oblong, spread with softened butter, sprinkle on sugar and dried fruit.
5. Roll up like a Swiss roll, cut into portions and put on to warm tray or in the tin (this gives better shaped buns).
6. Prove for 20 minutes, then bake for time and temperature given until golden brown.
7. Blend water and sugar and brush over the buns. The buns may be reheated to freshen them.

Croissants

Cooking time: 15–20 minutes
Preparation time: 40 minutes plus time for dough to stand and prove
Main cooking utensil: flat baking tray or sheet
Oven temperature: hot (425–450°F., 220–230°C., Gas Mark 7–8)
Oven position: above centre
Makes: 12 rolls

Imperial
1 teaspoon sugar
$\frac{1}{2}$ pint less 4 tablespoons warm water
1 oz. fresh yeast or 1 tablespoon dried yeast
1 lb. plain flour
1–2 level teaspoons salt
1 oz. lard or butter
1 egg
4 oz. margarine or butter
Glaze:
beaten egg

Metric
1 teaspoon sugar
200 ml. warm water
25 g. fresh yeast or 1 tablespoon dried yeast
400 g. plain flour
1–2 level teaspoons salt
25 g. lard or butter
1 egg
100 g. margarine or butter
Glaze:
beaten egg

1. Prepare the yeast liquid as on page 9.
2. Sieve flour and salt, rub in lard then add the yeast liquid and egg.
3. Knead until the dough is very smooth.
4. Roll dough into long strip about 20 inches (50 cm.) by 6 inches (15 cm.) by $\frac{1}{4}$ inch ($\frac{1}{2}$ cm.) thick.
5. Divide margarine into three, then cover two-thirds of the dough with one part of the margarine.
6. Fold in three, bring plain part up first and bottom part down.
7. Turn at right angles, seal ends, then roll and repeat twice with rest of margarine. Put away in cool place for 10 minutes then roll and fold three times more.
8. Leave in cool place for 1 hour, then roll out to oblong shape, and cut into twelve triangles.
9. To shape croissants, twist triangles towards point and form into a crescent.
10. Put on baking tray, brush with egg.
11. Allow to prove for 30 minutes until double in size then bake for time and at temperature given. Serve fresh and hot.

Devonshire cream scones and Cream cheese scones

Cooking time: 12–15 minutes
Preparation time: 10 minutes
Main cooking utensils: flat baking trays or sheets, 1½- to 2-inch (4- to 5-cm.) pastry cutter
Oven temperature: hot to very hot (450–475°F., 230–240°C., Gas Mark 8–9)
Oven position: near top

Devonshire cream scones

Imperial	Metric
8 oz. flour (with plain flour use 2 teaspoons baking powder)	200 g flour (with plain flour use 2 teaspoons baking powder)
pinch salt	pinch salt
$\frac{1}{4}$ teaspoon cream of tartar	$\frac{1}{4}$ teaspoon cream of tartar
3 oz. butter	75 g. butter
1 egg	1 egg
scant $\frac{1}{4}$ pint top of milk	120 ml. top of milk
1 tablespoon cream	1 tablespoon cream
Glaze:	*Glaze:*
beaten egg	beaten egg

1. Sieve all dry ingredients together.
2. Rub in the butter.
3. Add beaten egg and milk and cream.
4. Knead lightly, press or roll out until $\frac{3}{4}$ to 1 inch (2 to $2\frac{1}{2}$ cm.) thick on a floured board.
5. Cut into rounds, put on baking sheets.
6. Brush over with beaten egg.
7. Bake for time and at temperature given until firm to the touch. Serve hot or cold, split and buttered, with Devonshire cream and strawberry jam.

Cream cheese scones

Imperial	Metric
8 oz. flour (with plain flour use 2 teaspoons baking powder)	200 g. flour (with plain flour use 2 teaspoons baking powder)
pinch salt	pinch salt
2 oz. butter	50 g. butter
3 oz. sour cream cheese or cottage cheese	75 g. sour cream cheese or cottage cheese
1 egg	1 egg
$\frac{1}{4}$ pint milk	125 ml. milk

1. Sieve all dry ingredients together.
2. Rub in butter, then mix in the cheese and the beaten egg.
3. Add milk gradually until a smooth dough is formed.
4. Roll out and cut into shapes, place on baking sheet.
5. Bake as the Devonshire cream scones. Serve with butter.

Variation

Top Cream cheese scones with milk and cracked wheat before baking.

Cheese and bacon scones

Cooking time: 12–15 minutes
Preparation time: 10 minutes
Main cooking utensils: 2-inch (5-cm.) pastry cutter, flat baking tray or sheet
Oven temperature: hot (425°F., 220°C., Gas Mark 7)
Oven position: near top
Makes: 12–14 scones

Imperial

8 oz. self-raising flour
2 level teaspoons baking powder
½ level teaspoon dry mustard
¼ level teaspoon salt
pinch pepper
2 oz. margarine
3 oz. cheese, finely grated
3 rashers bacon, cooked and finely chopped
6–7 tablespoons milk
Glaze:
egg yolk

Metric

200 g. self-raising flour
2 level teaspoons baking powder
½ level teaspoon dry mustard
¼ level teaspoon salt
pinch pepper
50 g. margarine
75 g. cheese, finely grated
3 rashers bacon, cooked and finely chopped
6–7 tablespoons milk
Glaze:
egg yolk

1. Sieve the flour, baking powder, mustard, salt and pepper together.
2. Place all the ingredients in a bowl.
3. Mix together thoroughly with a wooden spoon to form a dough.
4. Turn out on to a lightly floured board.
5. Roll out to ½-inch (1-cm.) thickness.
6. Cut into rounds.
7. Place on baking tray and brush the tops with egg yolk.
8. Bake for time and temperature given.
9. Cool on a wire tray.
10. Split and top with a savoury butter, or butter.

Savoury butter

Add chopped parsley and a little lemon juice or chopped watercress and a little lemon juice to butter.

Note: This method of scone making is only applicable when using a luxury quick creaming margarine. This recipe needs more baking powder than usual. With plain flour use 4 level teaspoons baking powder. When baking always check oven temperature with that recommended in your cooker instruction card or book.

Cheese scone round

Cooking time: 10–15 minutes
Preparation time: 15 minutes
Main cooking utensil: baking tray or sheet, 2-inch (5-cm.) pastry cutter
Oven temperature: hot (425–450°F., 220–230°C., Gas Mark 7–8)
Oven position: above centre
Serves: 8

Imperial	Metric
8 oz. plain flour	200 g. plain flour
4 level teaspoons baking powder	4 level teaspoons baking powder
$\frac{1}{2}$ level teaspoon salt	$\frac{1}{2}$ level teaspoon salt
pinch dry mustard	pinch dry mustard
2 oz. butter	50 g. butter
4 oz. grated Cheddar cheese	100 g. grated Cheddar cheese
about $\frac{1}{4}$ pint milk	about 125 ml. milk
Glaze:	*Glaze:*
1 egg	1 egg
Topping:	*Topping:*
1 oz. grated Cheddar cheese	25 g. grated Cheddar cheese

1. Sieve the flour, baking powder, salt and mustard together and rub in the butter.
2. Add the grated cheese and sufficient milk to make a soft dough.
3. Knead lightly and roll out to 1-inch (2-cm.) thickness.
4. Cut out rounds with the pastry cutter.
5. Arrange the scones in a ring of eight, on a lightly floured baking sheet.
6. Brush with egg on top and where they touch one another.
7. Sprinkle grated cheese on top.
8. Bake for time and temperature given until well risen and golden brown. Serve them hot or cold at any meal. They make a pleasant change from bread rolls with soup or the main course.

Variation

Use $\frac{1}{4}$ pint (125 ml.) tomato juice in place of milk or add a little Marmite (yeast extract) to the milk to flavour.

Hot apple muffins

Cooking time: 25 minutes
Preparation time: 20
Main cooking utensils: muffin tins (deep patty tins)
Oven temperature: moderate (350–375°F., 180–190°C., Gas Mark 4–5)
Oven position: towards top
Makes: 24 muffins

Imperial	Metric
8 oz. flour (with plain flour use 3 level teaspoons baking powder, or with self-raising flour use 1 level teaspoon baking powder)	200 g. flour (with plain flour use 3 level teaspoons baking powder, or with self-raising flour use 1 level teaspoon baking powder)
$\frac{1}{2}$ teaspoon salt	$\frac{1}{2}$ teaspoon salt
$\frac{1}{4}$ teaspoon cinnamon	$\frac{1}{4}$ teaspoon cinnamon
$\frac{3}{4}$ teaspoon nutmeg	$\frac{3}{4}$ teaspoon nutmeg
2 beaten eggs	2 beaten eggs
$\frac{1}{2}$ pint milk	250 ml. milk
2 tablespoons melted butter	2 tablespoons melted butter
3 oz. castor sugar	75 g. castor sugar
2 medium-sized apples	2 medium-sized apples
Decoration:	*Decoration:*
1 apple	1 apple
little sugar	little sugar
little cinnamon	little cinnamon

1. Sieve together the flour, baking powder, salt, cinnamon and nutmeg.
2. Combine the beaten eggs, milk and melted butter.
3. Add the sugar and pour over dry ingredients and stir until they are moistened.
4. Stir in the chopped apples.
5. Fill the greased muffin tins two-thirds full with batter.
6. Decorate each muffin with two apple slices and dust with a mixture of sugar and cinnamon.
7. Bake for time and temperature given. Serve hot with butter. These do not keep.

Variation

Ginger muffins: Recipe as above but use 1 teaspoon powdered ginger instead of cinnamon and nutmeg, omit the apples and decorate with pieces of crystallised or well-drained preserved ginger before baking.

American ring doughnuts

Cooking time: about 3 minutes each batch
Preparation time: 15 minutes
Main cooking utensils: 2-inch (5-cm.) cutter, 1-inch ($2\frac{1}{2}$-cm.) cutter, pan for fat (with frying basket if possible)
Makes: 12–15 doughnuts

Imperial	Metric
12 oz. self-raising flour or 12 oz. plain flour with 2 level teaspoons cream of tartar and 1 level teaspoon bicarbonate of soda	300 g. self-raising flour or 300 g. plain flour with 2 level teaspoons cream of tartar and 1 level teaspoon bicarbonate of soda
½ teaspoon cinnamon	½ teaspoon cinnamon
½ teaspoon mixed spice	½ teaspoon mixed spice
4 oz. margarine	100 g. margarine
3 oz. castor sugar	75 g. castor sugar
1 egg	1 egg
6 tablespoons milk	6 tablespoons milk
1½ lb. fat for frying (should give 3-inch depth in pan)	675 g. fat for frying (should give 7-cm. depth in pan)
Coating:	*Coating:*
castor sugar	castor sugar

1. Sieve together the flour with the dry ingredients.
2. Rub in the margarine until the mixture looks like fine breadcrumbs, add sugar.
3. Stir in the beaten egg and enough milk to give a soft but not sticky, dough.
4. Turn out on to a lightly floured board, knead lightly, then roll out to ¾-inch (1½-cm.) thickness.
5. Cut into 2-inch (5-cm.) rounds, then with the smaller cutter remove the centres.
6. Gather up the parts removed, knead quickly, roll out and continue as 5.
7. Heat the fat to 360°F. (182°C.) or until a cube of bread a day old turns golden in 1 minute.
8. Put in one batch of doughnut rings, fry steadily until golden brown.
9. Lift out, drain on absorbent paper. Roll in castor sugar. Continue like this with each batch. Serve with hot coffee or chocolate.

Variation

Omit spices and roll into balls. This means longer cooking, so reduce the heat when frying.

Oaties

Cooking time: 20 minutes
Preparation time: 15 minutes
Main cooking utensils: saucepan, 7-inch (18-cm.) sandwich tin
Oven temperature: moderate (350–375°F., 180–190°C., Gas Mark 4–5)
Oven position: just above centre
Makes: 8 oaties

Imperial	**Metric**
4 oz. plain flour	100 g. plain flour
2 level teaspoons baking powder	2 level teaspoons baking powder
½ level teaspoon salt	½ level teaspoon salt
4 oz. rolled oats	100 g. rolled oats
2 oz. castor sugar	50 g. castor sugar
3 oz. black treacle	75 g. black treacle
4 oz. butter or margarine	100 g. butter or margarine
Decoration:	*Decoration:*
little coarse oatmeal or almond nibs	little coarse oatmeal or almond nibs

1. Sieve the flour, baking powder and salt together. Add the rolled oats.
2. Put the sugar, black treacle and butter or margarine into a saucepan and heat until just melted.
3. Mix this into the flour and stir until all the ingredients are thoroughly combined.
4. Press into the greased sandwich tin.
5. Sprinkle the surface of the oaties with coarse oatmeal.
6. Bake for time and at temperature given until firm to the touch.
7. Cut into wedges before the mixture cools. These are excellent for breakfast or for tea, and are delicious split and toasted and spread with butter.

Note: Any basic scone recipe may be used with 50% flour, 50% fine or medium oatmeal – better in this case than rolled oats.

Variation

Use syrup or honey in place of treacle.

Rock buns

Cooking time: 12–15 minutes
Preparation time: 10 minutes
Main cooking utensils: 2 baking trays or sheets
Oven temperature: hot (425–450°F., 220–230°C., Gas Mark 7–8)
Oven position: above centre
Makes: 10–12 buns

Imperial	Metric
8 oz. self-raising flour (with plain flour 2 level teaspoons baking powder)	200 g. self-raising flour (with plain flour 2 level teaspoons baking powder)
4 oz. lard	100 g. lard
4 oz. sugar	100 g. sugar
4 oz. dried fruit	100 g. dried fruit
1 egg	1 egg
milk to mix	milk to mix
little castor sugar	little castor sugar
Decoration:	*Decoration:*
little castor sugar	little castor sugar

1. Sieve the flour or flour and baking powder.
2. Rub in the lard until it resembles fine breadcrumbs, add the sugar and fruit.
3. Stir in the beaten egg and enough milk to make a sticky consistency.
4. Drop the mixture in small heaps on the greased trays, allowing room for cakes to spread during cooking; sprinkle with sugar lightly before baking.
5. Cook for time and at temperature given until crisp and golden brown.
6. Lift carefully on to a wire cooling tray for cakes are fragile when hot. Sprinkle with more sugar; eat with tea or coffee.

Note: A sticky mixture stands up in peaks when handled with a knife. A slow dropping consistency needs a shake to remove from spoon.

Variation
Add chopped peel, grated rind of fresh orange or lemon.

Raisin bread

Cooking time: 50–60 minutes
Preparation time: 20 minutes
Main cooking utensil: 2-lb. (1-kg.) loaf tin
Oven temperature: moderate (350–375°F., 180–190°C., Gas Mark 4–5)
Oven position: centre
Makes: 20 slices

Imperial
6 oz. seedless raisins
8 oz. plain flour
2 level teaspoons baking powder
½ level teaspoon bicarbonate of soda
½ level teaspoon salt
3 oz. rolled oats
2 oz. butter
2 oz. sugar
1 egg
½ pint sour milk (or 1 level teaspoon cream of tartar with fresh milk)

Metric
150 g. seedless raisins
200 g. plain flour
2 level teaspoons baking powder
½ level teaspoon bicarbonate of soda
½ level teaspoon salt
75 g. rolled oats
50 g. butter
50 g. sugar
1 egg
250 ml. sour milk (or 1 level teaspoon cream of tartar with fresh milk)

1. Plump the raisins by covering with cold water, bringing to the boil and standing for five minutes. Drain very well.
2. Sieve the dry ingredients, add the rolled oats and raisins.
3. Cream the butter and sugar until light and fluffy, beat in the egg gradually.
4. Add dry ingredients alternately with the sour milk to make a soft dough.
5. Place in the greased and floured loaf tin and bake until firm. Serve sliced fairly thickly and spread with butter.

Note: When baking always check oven temperature with that recommended in your cooker instruction card or book. If using raisins with seeds, remove the seeds by breaking the raisins with your fingers or halving with a knife. Take out the seeds with damp fingers. If the fruit becomes wet, use slightly less milk.

Variation
Add the grated rind of an orange and the juice in place of some of the sour milk.

Wholemeal date loaf

Cooking time: 1 hour
Preparation time: 15 minutes
Main cooking utensil: 1-lb. (½-kg.) loaf tin
Oven temperature: moderate (375°F., 190°C., Gas Mark 5)
Oven position: centre
Serves: 8

Imperial
4 oz. wholemeal flour
4 oz. plain flour
2 level teaspoons baking powder
2 oz. margarine
6 oz. dates, stoned
1 egg
2 tablespoons golden syrup
7 tablespoons milk

Metric
100 g. wholemeal flour
100 g. plain flour
2 level teaspoons baking powder
50 g. margarine
150 g. dates, stoned
1 egg
2 tablespoons golden syrup
7 tablespoons milk

1. Sieve flours and baking powder into a bowl.
2. Rub in the margarine until the mixture resembles fine breadcrumbs.
3. Add the chopped dates and mix thoroughly.
4. Stir in the rest of the ingredients.
5. Place the mixture in a greased loaf tin. Smooth the top.
6. Bake for time and at temperature given until firm to the touch.
7. Leave in the tin for 2–3 minutes before turning out on to a wire tray to cool. Serve sliced and spread with butter.

Note: If making wholemeal bread for the first time, be prepared for it to take longer in cooking than white bread since it absorbs more moisture. It is therefore advisable to use a slightly lower oven temperature.
When baking always check oven temperatures with that recommended in your cooker instruction card or book.

Variation
Use mixed dried fruit instead of dates.

Soda bread

Cooking time: 25–30 minutes
Preparation time: 10 minutes
Main cooking utensil: flat baking tray or sheet
Oven temperature: very hot (475°F., 240°C., Gas Mark 9), then moderately hot (400°F., 200°C., Gas Mark 6)
Oven position: centre
Serves: 4

Imperial
1 oz. margarine, optional
8 oz. plain flour
pinch salt
1 level teaspoon bicarbonate of soda
$\frac{1}{4}$ pint sour milk or fresh milk with 1 teaspoon cream of tartar
Glaze:
little milk

Metric
25 g. margarine, optional
200 g. plain flour
pinch salt
1 level teaspoon bicarbonate of soda
125 ml. sour milk or fresh milk with 1 teaspoon cream of tartar
Glaze:
little milk

1. Rub the margarine into the flour (this is not essential, but helps to keep the bread moist).
2. Add the salt, dissolve the bicarbonate of soda in the sour milk, add to the flour.
3. Knead lightly and form into a round loaf.
4. Brush with a little milk.
5. Bake for 15 minutes in a very hot oven then lower the heat to moderately hot for a further 10–15 minutes until the bread is firm to the touch. Serve when fresh with butter.

Note: You can use self-raising flour and fresh milk instead of plain flour and sour milk.

Variation
Raisin soda bread: Add 4 oz. (100 g.) seedless raisins to the flour, add $\frac{1}{2}$–1 teaspoon caraway seeds if wished. Form into a round. Brush top of the bread with melted butter, sprinkle with castor sugar and mark into four portions before cooking.

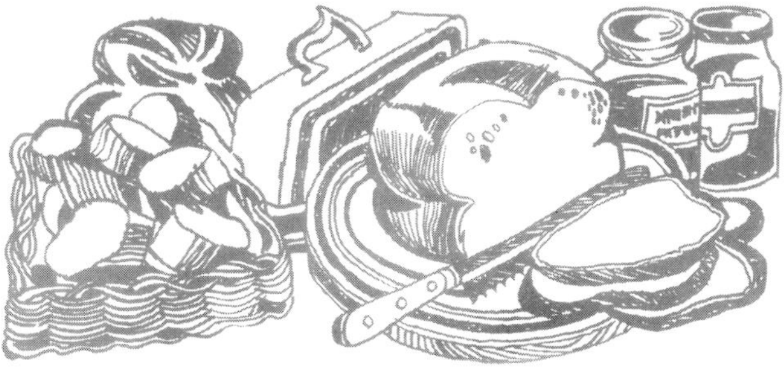

Honey squares

Cooking time: 30 minutes
Preparation time: 20 minutes
Main cooking utensil: 7-inch (18-cm.) square baking tin, lined with greased paper
Oven temperature: moderate (375°F., 190°C., Gas Mark 5)
Oven position: just above centre
Makes: 9–12 squares

Imperial
4 oz. plain flour
pinch salt
1 teaspoon powdered ginger
1 teaspoon cinnamon
1 level teaspoon bicarbonate of soda
3 tablespoons oil
2 oz. honey
2 oz. black treacle
2 oz. Demerara sugar
1 egg
2 tablespoons milk
2 oz. sultanas
Decoration:
2 oz. walnuts or almonds

Metric
100 g. plain flour
pinch salt
1 teaspoon powdered ginger
1 teaspoon cinnamon
1 level teaspoon bicarbonate of soda
3 tablespoons oil
50 g. honey
50 g. black treacle
50 g. Demerara sugar
1 egg
2 tablespoons milk
50 g. sultanas
Decoration:
50 g. walnuts or almonds

1. Sieve together the dry ingredients.
2. Add the oil, honey, treacle and sugar.
3. Beat well, then stir in the egg and milk and beat again.
4. Lastly add the sultanas.
5. Put into the prepared tin and top with the coarsely chopped nuts.
6. Bake until firm to the touch – cool well before cutting. Cut into squares as a cake when very fresh or split and butter.

Variation
Use all honey and omit the treacle or use golden syrup instead of treacle; add 2 oz. (50 g.) chopped nuts.

Cream buns

Cooking time: 30–45 minutes
Preparation time: 20 minutes
Main cooking utensils: small saucepan, baking tray or deep roasting tin
Oven temperature: hot (425°F., 220°C., Gas Mark 6)
Oven position: centre
Makes: 14–16 small or 8–10 larger buns

Imperial

Choux pastry:
2 oz. self-raising flour
pinch salt
$\frac{1}{8}$ pint water (about 4 tablespoons)
1 oz. butter or margarine
1–2 eggs
Filling:
8–12 oz. strawberries
just over $\frac{1}{4}$ pint cream
1–2 tablespoons castor sugar

Metric

Choux pastry:
50 g. self-raising flour
pinch salt
70 ml. water (about 4 tablespoons)
25 g. butter or margarine
1–2 eggs
Filling:
200–300 g. strawberries
150 ml. cream
1–2 tablespoons castor sugar

1. Sieve the flour and salt.
2. Bring the water and fat to the boil, add the flour. Stir quickly with a wooden spoon until mixture forms a smooth ball of dough.
3. Remove from heat, beat in 1 egg thoroughly until absorbed. Beat second egg, add sufficient to bring mixture to a velvety consistency, keeping its shape when pulled into points with a spoon. Beat thoroughly.
4. Either pipe rounds of the choux pastry on to a greased tray or put spoonfuls on the tray. Allow plenty of room for the mixture to spread.
5. If possible bake in a deep cake or roasting tin and cover the top with another tin or foil – this produces a better shape.
6. Bake the buns allowing approximately 25–30 minutes if uncovered, 30–45 minutes if covered (depending on size).
7. Allow buns to cool away from draught. Split, dry out for a few minutes if necessary. Serve filled with fruit and cream, dust with icing sugar.

Sticky gingerbread

Cooking time: $1\frac{1}{4}$–$1\frac{1}{2}$ hours
Preparation time: 10 minutes
Main cooking utensils: large saucepan, 7-inch (18-cm.) square tin, greaseproof paper
Oven temperature: slow (300–325°F., 150–170°C., Gas Mark 2–3)
Oven position: centre
Makes: 12 pieces

Imperial

4 oz. margarine or lard
6 oz. black treacle and 2 oz. golden syrup or use all black treacle
¼ pint milk
8 oz. plain flour
2 oz. brown sugar
1 level teaspoon mixed spice
1 level teaspoon bicarbonate of soda
1–2 level teaspoons ground ginger
2 eggs

Metric

100 g. margarine or lard
150 g. black treacle and 50 g. golden syrup or use all black treacle
125 ml. milk
200 g. plain flour
50 g. brown sugar
1 level teaspoon mixed spice
1 level teaspoon bicarbonate of soda
1–2 level teaspoons ground ginger
2 eggs

1. Warm the margarine or lard, black treacle and syrup.
2. Add the milk and allow to cool.
3. Sieve the dry ingredients into a bowl, add the treacle mixture and the eggs; beat well.
4. Pour into a lined tin.
5. Bake for time and at temperature given until firm to touch.

Note: Try to make gingerbread several days before cutting. The parkin (see below) can be eaten fresh.

Variation

Yorkshire parkin: Use 3 oz. (75 g.) lard instead of 4 oz. (100 g.), use 4 oz. (100 g.) plain flour and 4 oz. (100 g.) medium oatmeal or rolled oats and ¼ level teaspoon salt in place of 8 oz. (200 g.) flour. Make stiffer with 1 egg and 5 tablespoons milk only.

Blueberry bread

Cooking time: 1 hour
Preparation time: 25 minutes
Main cooking utensil: 2-lb. (1-kg.) loaf tin
Oven temperature: very moderate (325–350°F., 170–180°C., Gas Mark 3–4)
Oven position: centre
Makes: 1 large loaf

Imperial	Metric
10 oz. plain flour	250 g. plain flour
1 level teaspoon baking powder	1 level teaspoon baking powder
1 level teaspoon bicarbonate of soda	1 level teaspoon bicarbonate of soda
pinch salt	pinch salt
½ teaspoon grated nutmeg	½ teaspoon grated nutmeg
2 oz. quick cooking oats	50 g. quick cooking oats
3 oz. softened butter	75 g. softened butter
4 oz. light brown sugar	100 g. light brown sugar
2 eggs	2 eggs
½ pint buttermilk	250 ml. buttermilk
4 oz. chopped walnuts	100 g. chopped walnuts
4–6 oz. fresh or frozen blueberries	100–150 g. fresh or frozen blueberries
¼ pint thick apple purée	125 ml. thick apple purée

1. Sieve flour with baking powder, bicarbonate of soda, salt and nutmeg.
2. Stir in raw rolled oats.
3. In another bowl cream together the butter and brown sugar.
4. Beat in the eggs, add buttermilk.
5. Make a well in centre of the flour mixture and pour in egg mixture.
6. Stir until dry ingredients are moistened and well blended.
7. Fold in nuts, the raw or drained defrosted blueberries and the apple purée.
8. Turn batter into greased tin and spread evenly.
9. Bake for time and at temperature given until the loaf is golden brown and firm to the touch, then cool. Serve cold with butter.

Note: Instead of buttermilk you could use fresh milk and a few drops of vinegar.

Variation

Other berry fruits could be used instead of blueberries.

Glazed cherry bread

Cooking time: 1 hour
Preparation time: 20 minutes
Main cooking utensils: saucepan, 2 1-lb. ($\frac{1}{2}$-kg.) loaf tins
Oven temperature: very moderate (325–350°F., 170–180°C., Gas Mark 3–4)
Oven position: centre
Makes: 2 small loaves

Imperial	Metric
12 oz. flour (with plain flour use 3 level teaspoons baking powder)	300 g. flour (with plain flour use 3 level teaspoons baking powder)
$\frac{1}{2}$ level teaspoon salt	$\frac{1}{2}$ level teaspoon salt
2 oz. castor sugar	50 g. castor sugar
2 oz. walnuts	50 g. walnuts
2 oz. dates	50 g. dates
3 level tablespoons malt extract	3 level tablespoons malt extract
2 oz. butter or margarine	50 g. butter or margarine
$\frac{1}{4}$ pint milk	125 ml. milk
2 eggs	2 eggs
Glaze:	*Glaze:*
2 oz. castor sugar	50 g. castor sugar
2 tablespoons water	2 tablespoons water
Decoration:	*Decoration:*
1 oz. walnuts	25 g. walnuts
$1\frac{1}{2}$ oz. glacé cherries	40 g. glacé cherries

1. Sieve the flour and salt into a bowl.
2. Add the sugar, chopped walnuts and stoned and chopped dates.
3. Gently heat the malt and butter or margarine until the fat has melted.
4. Pour into the centre of the flour mixture with blended milk and eggs.
5. Mix together to a smooth, soft dough.
6. Put into 2 greased and floured tins.
7. Bake for time and at temperature given until firm to the touch.
8. Turn on to a wire cooling tray, glaze while hot.
9. To make the glaze, heat the sugar and water in a pan and boil for 2–3 minutes until syrupy.
10. Decorate with nuts and halved cherries. Serve sliced for tea. This needs no butter although it can be used.

Variation

Use raisins in place of dates.

Canadian apple nut bread

Cooking time: 1 hour
Preparation time: 20 minutes
Main cooking utensil: 2-lb. (1-kg.) loaf tin
Oven temperature: very moderate (325–350°F., 170–180°C., Gas Mark 3–4)
Oven position: centre
Serves: 10–12

Imperial

7 oz. flour (with plain flour use 2½ level teaspoons baking powder, with self-raising flour use 1 level teaspoon baking powder)
½ level teaspoon cinnamon
pinch nutmeg
½ teaspoon salt
2 oz. chopped walnuts
3 oz. butter
5 oz. sugar
2 eggs
2 tablespoons milk
1 diced cooking apple
1½ oz. seedless raisins
Glacé icing:
4 oz. sieved icing sugar
1½ dessertspoons warm water
Decoration:
stewed apples
chopped nuts

Metric

175 g. flour (with plain flour use 2½ level teaspoons baking powder, with self-raising flour use 1 level teaspoon baking powder)
½ level teaspoon cinnamon
pinch nutmeg
½ teaspoon salt
50 g. chopped walnuts
75 g. butter
125 g. sugar
2 eggs
2 tablespoons milk
1 diced cooking apple
40 g. seedless raisins
Glacé icing:
100 g. sieved icing sugar
1½ dessertspoons warm water
Decoration:
stewed apples
chopped nuts

1. Sieve the dry ingredients together and add the nuts.
2. Cream the butter and sugar together until fluffy, and beat in the eggs.
3. Add the dry ingredients alternately with the milk.
4. Stir in the apple and raisins, pour into a greased loaf tin.
5. Bake for time and at temperature given until firm to the touch.
6. To make the glacé icing blend the sieved icing sugar and warmed water. Spread over the top of the bread and allow it to trickle down the sides. Decorate with sliced apples and nuts.

Variation

Use other nuts in place of walnuts, glacé cherries, angelica.

American apple cake

Cooking time: 25 minutes
Preparation time: 15 minutes
Main cooking utensil: Swiss roll tin, approximately 7 by 10 inches (18 by 25 cm.)
Oven temperature: moderately hot to hot (425°F., 220°C., Gas Mark 7)
Oven position: just above centre
Serves: 12

Imperial	Metric
10 oz. self-raising flour	250 g. self-raising flour
1 level teaspoon baking powder	1 level teaspoon baking powder
1 oz. castor sugar	25 g. castor sugar
$\frac{3}{4}$ teaspoon salt	$\frac{3}{4}$ teaspoon salt
4 oz. butter or margarine	100 g. butter or margarine
2 oz. grated cheese	50 g. grated cheese
about $\frac{1}{4}$ pint milk	about 125 ml. milk
4 eating apples	4 eating apples
2–3 oz. brown sugar	50–75 g. brown sugar
$\frac{1}{2}$ teaspoon cinnamon	$\frac{1}{2}$ teaspoon cinnamon
1 tablespoon melted butter	1 tablespoon melted butter

1. Sift flour, baking powder, castor sugar and salt together.
2. Rub in butter or margarine and then mix in cheese.
3. Add sufficient milk to make a soft but not sticky dough.
4. Turn on to a floured board and knead dough lightly.
5. Pat out dough in ungreased Swiss roll tin.
6. Pare and core apples, slice thinly.
7. Arrange in rows across dough.
8. Sprinkle with brown sugar and cinnamon mixed together.
9. Brush over with melted butter.
10. Bake for time and at temperature given. Serve sliced with coffee.

Note: When baking always check oven temperatures with that recommended in your cooker instruction card or book.

Variation

Use fresh apricots.

Sultana loaf

Cooking time: $1\frac{1}{4}$ hours
Preparation time: 20 minutes
Main cooking utensil: 2-lb. (1-kg.) loaf tin
Oven temperature: moderate (350°F., 180°C., Gas Mark 4)
Oven position: centre
Serves: 8

Imperial	Metric
8 oz. self-raising flour (or plain flour with 2 level teaspoons baking powder)	200 g. self-raising flour (or plain flour with 2 level teaspoons baking powder)
4 oz. butter	100 g. butter
4 oz. castor sugar	100 g. castor sugar
2 eggs	2 eggs
6 oz. sultanas	150 g. sultanas
milk to mix	milk to mix
Decoration:	*Decoration:*
4–6 oz. sieved icing sugar	100–150 g. sieved icing sugar
$1\frac{1}{2}$ dessertspoons water	$1\frac{1}{2}$ dessertspoons water
12 walnut halves	12 walnut halves
1–2 oz. sultanas	25–50 g. sultanas

1. Sieve flour into a basin.
2. Cream butter and sugar in a bowl until light and fluffy.
3. Add eggs one by one, beating well. If mixture curdles, add little of the flour.
4. Fold in half the flour, then the fruit.
5. Add rest of the flour and enough milk to give a soft dropping consistency.
6. Turn mixture into the greased tin.
7. Bake in the oven until cooked and firm to the touch.
8. Turn on to a wire cooling tray and cool.
9. Blend icing sugar with the water.
10. Spread over cake and decorate with the walnuts and sultanas. Serve with tea or coffee, cut in slices.

Variation
Flavour with grated orange or lemon rind.

Speedy orange cake

Cooking time: 55 minutes
Preparation time: 10 minutes
Main cooking utensil: 6-inch (15-cm.) square or 7-inch (18-cm.) round cake tin
Oven temperature: moderate (350–375°F., 180–190°C., Gas Mark 4–5)
Oven position: centre
Serves: 8

Imperial
5 oz. sieved self-raising flour
4 oz. castor sugar
3 oz. shortening (lightened cooking fat)
2 eggs
1 tablespoon orange juice
grated rind of 1 orange

Metric
125 g. sieved self-raising flour
100 g. castor sugar
75 g. shortening (lightened cooking fat)
2 eggs
1 tablespoon orange juice
grated rind of 1 orange

1. Put all ingredients into a large mixing bowl and stir gently until softened then cream briskly for about 2 minutes until soft and light.
2. Put the mixture into a greased and floured cake tin and flatten the top.
3. Bake for time and at temperature given.
4. Test cake before removing from the oven. It is cooked when shrunk away from the tin and when no impression is left when it is pressed gently but firmly on top with the finger.
5. Turn out and cool on a wire tray. Serve cut in slices.

Note: This method of mixing is only suitable for modern shortening or quick creaming margarine. The same proportion of ingredients can be used with butter or ordinary margarine but it is then important to cream the butter and sugar in the usual way.

Variation
Use lemon rind and juice in place of orange.

Spiced honey cake

Cooking time: $1\frac{1}{4}$ hours
Preparation time: 20 minutes
Main cooking utensils: pan, 2-lb. (1-kg.) loaf tin lined with greased paper
Oven temperature: very moderate to moderate (350°F., 180°C., Gas Mark 4)
Oven position: centre
Makes: 1 loaf

Imperial	Metric
2 oz. butter	50 g. butter
5 oz. honey	125 g. honey
5 oz. Demerara sugar	125 g. Demerara sugar
10 oz. plain flour	250 g. plain flour
pinch salt	pinch salt
1 teaspoon baking powder	1 teaspoon baking powder
1 level teaspoon bicarbonate of soda	1 level teaspoon bicarbonate of soda
1 teaspoon mixed spice	1 teaspoon mixed spice
1 teaspoon powdered ginger	1 teaspoon powdered ginger
1 teaspoon cinnamon	1 teaspoon cinnamon
2–4 oz. chopped peel	50–100 g. chopped peel
1 egg	1 egg
$\frac{1}{4}$ pint milk	125 ml. milk
Decoration:	*Decoration:*
flaked almonds	flaked almonds

1. Heat the butter in the pan, then stir in the honey and sugar, allow to cool.
2. Sieve the flour, salt and baking powder and bicarbonate of soda.
3. Add the rest of the ingredients and beat very well until quite smooth.
4. Put into the prepared tin and top with almonds.
5. Bake until firm to the touch – look at the loaf after about $\frac{3}{4}$ hour and if browning too quickly lower the heat slightly.
6. Turn out carefully, and allow to cool. Serve sliced and buttered. This loaf keeps well.

Note: To measure honey, dip the spoon in very hot water, shake dry then dip into the jar – 1 level tablespoon equals 1 oz. (25 g.); to weigh honey, flour the scale pans – the honey comes away easily then.

If using self-raising flour you do not need baking powder or bicarbonate of soda.

Honey, date and walnut cake and Honey loaf

Cooking time: 1–1¼ hours
Preparation time: 15 minutes
Main cooking utensils: 7-inch (18-cm.) square tin; saucepan, 2-lb. (1-kg.) loaf tin or shallow tin
Oven temperature: moderate (350–375°F., 180–190°C., Gas Mark 4–5)
Serves: 10–14

Honey, date and walnut cake

Imperial	Metric
8 oz. plain flour	200 g. plain flour
3 teaspoons baking powder	3 teaspoons baking powder
4 oz. butter or margarine	100 g. butter or margarine
4 oz. castor sugar	100 g. castor sugar
4 oz. sliced stoned dates	100 g. sliced stoned dates
1 oz. chopped walnuts	25 g. chopped walnuts
2 eggs	2 eggs
4 tablespoons milk	4 tablespoons milk
2 tablespoons clear honey	2 tablespoons clear honey

1. Sieve dry ingredients, rub in butter.
2. Add the rest of the ingredients.
3. Pour into a greased tin.
4. Bake for time and at temperature given until firm.

Honey loaf

Imperial	Metric
8 oz. plain flour	200 g. plain flour
1 teaspoon baking powder	1 teaspoon baking powder
1 teaspoon cinnamon	1 teaspoon cinnamon
½ teaspoon salt	½ teaspoon salt
4 oz. brown sugar	100 g. brown sugar
½ pint milk	250 ml. milk
½ oz. butter	15 g. butter
8 oz. honey	200 g. honey

1. Sieve together the dry ingredients and add the sugar.
2. Warm the milk, butter and honey.
3. Stir on to the dry ingredients and beat well.
4. Put into a floured tin and bake for time and at temperature given until firm to the touch.
5. Serve sliced and spread with butter.

Sand cake

Cooking time: $1\frac{1}{4}$ hours
Preparation time: 15 minutes
Main cooking utensil: 2-lb. (1-kg.) loaf tin
Oven temperature: moderate (375°F., 190°C., Gas Mark 5)
Oven position: centre
Serves: 8–10

Imperial	**Metric**
6 oz. butter	150 g. butter
6 oz. castor sugar	150 g. castor sugar
3 eggs	3 eggs
½ teaspoon vanilla essence	½ teaspoon vanilla essence
4 oz. cornflour	100 g. cornflour
4 oz. plain flour	100 g. plain flour
1 level teaspoon baking powder	1 level teaspoon baking powder
2–3 tablespoons milk to mix	2–3 tablespoons milk to mix

1. Cream the butter and sugar until soft and light, add beaten eggs, and vanilla essence.
2. Fold in cornflour sieved with flour and baking powder.
3. Lastly add milk to make a medium soft consistency.
4. Spread in a greased and lined tin.
5. Bake for time and at temperature given until firm. Serve cut in slices.

Note: When baking always check oven temperature with that recommended in your cooker instruction card or book.

Variation

Rice cake: Use 4 oz. (100 g.) plain flour, 1 level teaspoon baking powder, 4 oz. (100 g.) ground rice – omit cornflour.

Almond cake: Ingredients as recipe, plus 2 oz. (50 g.) ground almonds. Top with blanched almonds before baking.

Cherry cake

Cooking time: $1\frac{1}{4}$–$1\frac{1}{2}$ hours
Preparation time: 15 minutes
Main cooking utensil: 6- or 7-inch (15- or 18-cm.) cake tin
Oven temperature: very moderate (325–350°F., 170–180°C., Gas Mark 3–4)
Oven position: centre
Serves: 8–10

Imperial	Metric
4 oz. butter or margarine	100 g. butter or margarine
4 oz. castor sugar	100 g. castor sugar
2 eggs	2 eggs
few drops vanilla essence	few drops vanilla essence
6 oz. plain flour	150 g. plain flour
1 level teaspoon baking powder	1 level teaspoon baking powder
3–4 oz. glacé cherries	75–100 g. glacé cherries
$1\frac{1}{2}$ tablespoons milk	$1\frac{1}{2}$ tablespoons milk

1. Cream the butter and sugar until soft and light.
2. Whisk eggs and gradually beat them into the butter mixture, if the mixture shows signs of curdling add a little sieved flour.
3. Add vanilla essence, fold in sieved flour and baking powder gently with metal spoon.
4. Add the cherries. These should be halved or quartered and coated in flour. If very sticky they should be rinsed in cold water then dried to prevent them from sinking. Then add milk.
5. Put into the greased and floured or lined tin. Level the top.
6. Bake for time and at temperature given.
7. Test cake before removing from the tin. Ensure the cake has shrunk away from the sides of the tin and feels firm to the touch.

Variation

For a richer cake, use 5 oz. (125 g.) butter and 5 oz. (125 g.) sugar, 4 oz. (100 g.) glacé cherries, 2 oz. (50 g.) ground almonds and 6 oz. (150 g.) plain flour, and 3 eggs and no milk.

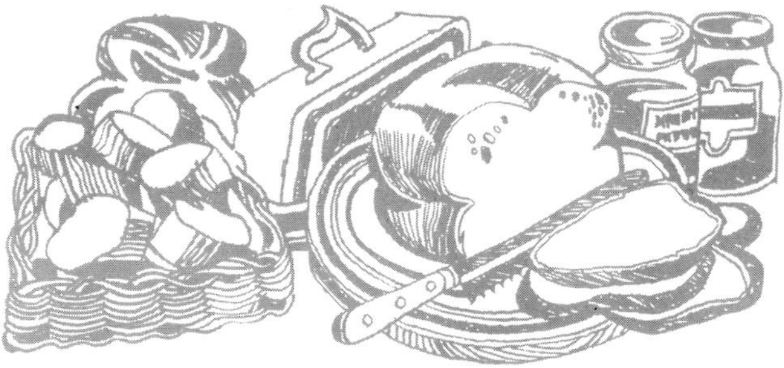

Apple cake

Cooking time: 1 hour
Preparation time: 20 minutes
Main cooking utensil: 7-inch (18-cm.) cake tin
Oven temperature: moderate to moderately hot (375–400°F., 190–200°C., Gas Mark 5–6)
Oven position: centre
Serves: 8

Imperial

8 oz. flour (with plain flour use 2 level teaspoons baking powder)
4 oz. margarine or lard
4 oz. sugar
1 egg, optional
8 oz. peeled apple (fairly sweet variety)
milk to mix
Decoration:
little brown sugar, optional

Metric

200 g. flour (with plain flour use 2 level teaspoons baking powder)
100 g. margarine or lard
100 g. sugar
1 egg, optional
200 g. peeled apple (fairly sweet variety)
milk to mix
Decoration:
little brown sugar, optional

1. Sieve the flour or flour and baking powder.
2. Rub in the margarine or lard until the mixture is like fine breadcrumbs.
3. Add the sugar and the egg if this is being used.
4. Cut the apple into neat dice, add this to the cake, mix well so that you have a good idea of its consistency.
5. Stir in enough milk to give a slow dropping consistency, i.e., the spoon needs a hard shake before the mixture drops back into the bowl.
6. Put into the greased tin.
7. Bake for time and at temperature given until firm to the touch; if the outside is browning too much reduce the heat slightly.
8. Turn out carefully and top with sugar.

Variation

Add a little spice and some currants.

Family fruit cake

Cooking time: 1–1$\frac{1}{4}$ hours
Preparation time: 10 minutes
Main cooking utensil: 2-lb. (1-kg.) loaf tin
Oven temperature: moderate (350–375°F., 180–190°C., Gas Mark 4–5)
Oven position: centre
Serves: 8–10

Imperial	Metric
8 oz. self-raising flour (or plain flour and 2 level teaspoons baking powder)	200 g. self-raising flour (or plain flour and 2 level teaspoons baking powder)
1 level teaspoon mixed spice	1 level teaspoon mixed spice
½ level teaspoon cinnamon	½ level teaspoon cinnamon
3–4 oz. butter or margarine	75–100 g. butter or margarine
3–4 oz. sugar	75–100 g. sugar
4 oz. currants	100 g. currants
4 oz. sultanas	100 g. sultanas
1 oz. mixed peel	25 g. mixed peel
1 egg	1 egg
about ¼ pint milk	about 125 ml. milk

1. Sieve the flour or flour and baking powder with the spice and cinnamon.
2. Rub in the butter or margarine until the mixture looks like fine breadcrumbs.
3. Add the sugar, dried fruit and peel.
4. Mix with egg and milk to form a soft consistency, i.e., so the mixture drops easily from a knife.
5. Put into the greased and floured loaf tin, making the mixture quite level on top.
6. Bake for the time and at temperature given.
7. Test the cake before removing from the tin. Ensure the cake has shrunk away from the sides of the tin, and when a fine skewer is inserted into the cake it should come out quite clean. Slice and serve. If any mixture is left and becomes cold spread with a little butter and use as bread.

Variation

Use 4–6 oz. (100–150 g.) chopped dates instead of currants and sultanas. Mix with cold tea instead of milk (this gives a very moist cake).

Economical light fruit cake

Cooking time: 1–1$\frac{1}{4}$ hours
Preparation time: 25 minutes
Main cooking utensil: 2-lb. (1-kg.) loaf tin or 7-inch (18-cm.) cake tin
Oven temperature: moderate (350–375°F., 180–190°C., Gas Mark 4–5)
Oven position: centre
Makes: 10–12 slices

Imperial	Metric
4 oz. margarine	100 g. margarine
4 oz. castor sugar	100 g. castor sugar
2 eggs	2 eggs
8 oz. flour (with plain flour use 2 level teaspoons baking powder)	200 g. flour (with plain flour use 2 level teaspoons baking powder)
8 oz. dried fruit	200 g. dried fruit
1–2 oz. chopped candied peel	25–50 g. chopped candied peel
milk to mix – about 6 tablespoons	milk to mix – about 6 tablespoons
Decoration:	*Decoration:*
1–2 oz. blanched shredded almonds (optional)	25–50 g. blanched shredded almonds (optional)

1. Follow method for Victoria sandwich (see page 83), stages 1 to 3.
2. After adding the flour stir in fruit, peel and enough milk to make a slow dropping consistency.
3. Put into the greased and floured tin, top with almonds if desired.
4. Bake for time and at temperature given; allow shorter time for a loaf tin since the cake tends to cook more quickly.
5. Test before removing from the oven. The cake should have shrunk away from the sides of the tin, feel firm to the touch, and if a warm fine skewer is inserted it should come away clean.

Variation

Economical Madeira cake: Use recipe above, omitting dried fruit etc. and flavouring with grated rind of 1 lemon, top with piece of candied peel halfway through cooking.

Rich Madeira cake: Use 6 oz. (150 g.) butter, 6 oz. (150 g.) sugar, 3 eggs and little milk or 4 eggs and no milk. Bake in very moderate oven (325–350°F., 170–180°C., Gas Mark 3–4) for about $1\frac{1}{4}$–$1\frac{1}{2}$ hours.

Chocolate walnut cake

Cooking time: 1 hour
Preparation time: 20 minutes
Main cooking utensil: 7-inch (18-cm.) cake tin
Oven temperature: moderate (375°F., 190°C., Gas Mark 5)
Oven position: centre
Serves: 10

Imperial	Metric
4 oz. chocolate	100 g. chocolate
4 tablespoons milk	4 tablespoons milk
2 oz. shelled walnuts	50 g. shelled walnuts
6 oz. margarine	150 g. margarine
6 oz. castor sugar	150 g. castor sugar
2 eggs	2 eggs
7 oz. self-raising flour (with plain flour use 2 level teaspoons baking powder)	175 g. self-raising flour (with plain flour use 2 level teaspoons baking powder)
2 oz. ground rice	50 g. ground rice
Decoration:	*Decoration:*
little castor sugar	little castor sugar

1. Cut the chocolate into small pieces.
2. Heat the milk and add the chocolate. Stir until dissolved.
3. Chop the walnuts keeping 5 whole for decoration.
4. Cream the margarine and sugar until soft and fluffy.
5. Gradually beat in the eggs.
6. Sieve the flour and ground rice.
7. Add gently to the creamed mixture, then add the milk and melted chocolate.
8. Add the chopped walnuts.
9. Put into a prepared tin.
10. Arrange whole walnuts on top.
11. Bake for time and at temperature given.
12. Test before removing from the oven. See that the cake has shrunk away from the sides of the tin and is firm to the touch.
13. Dredge well with castor sugar. Serve cut in slices. This cake keeps well in an airtight tin.

Note: When baking always check oven temperatures with that recommended in your cooker instruction card or book.

Variation

Mocha walnut cake: Dissolve the chocolate in strong coffee instead of milk.

Surprise cake

Cooking time: $1\frac{1}{4}$ hours
Preparation time: 30 minutes
Main cooking utensil: 7-inch (18-cm.) cake tin
Oven temperature: moderate (325–350°F., 170–180°C., Gas Mark 3–4)
Oven position: centre
Serves: 8–10

Imperial	Metric
5 oz. butter	125 g. butter
5 oz. castor sugar	125 g. castor sugar
3 eggs	3 eggs
8 oz. self-raising flour	200 g. self-raising flour
4 oz. (1 packet) Chocolate Polka Dots (chocolate chips)	100 g. Chocolate Polka Dots (chocolate chips)
1 tablespoon milk	1 tablespoon milk
Icing:	*Icing:*
4 oz. butter	100 g. butter
½ teaspoon vanilla essence	½ teaspoon vanilla essence
3 tablespoons evaporated milk	3 tablespoons evaporated milk
4 oz. (1 packet) Chocolate Polka Dots (chocolate chips)	100 g. Chocolate Polka Dots (chocolate chips)
1 lb. sieved icing sugar	400 g. sieved icing sugar

1. Cream the butter and sugar until soft and light.
2. Gradually add the beaten eggs, stir in a little sieved flour if the mixture shows signs of curdling.
3. Fold in the sieved flour and the Chocolate Polka Dots, lightly dusted with flour, plus 1 tablespoon milk.
4. Put into the greased and floured cake tin, bake for time and at temperature given until the cake is firm to touch.
5. To make the icing, put all the ingredients except icing sugar into a basin or the top of a double saucepan over very hot water, heat until the chocolate is melted, allow to cool, then beat in the icing sugar.
6. Spread over the top and sides of the cake, then swirl with a small flat-bladed knife.

Note: When baking always check oven temperatures with that recommended in your cooker instruction card or book.

Variation

Add 2–3 oz. (50–75 g.) chopped nuts and a little vanilla essence.

For a richer cake use 6 oz. (150 g.) butter and 7 oz. (175 g.) sugar.

Victoria sandwich

Cooking time: 20 minutes
Preparation time: 15 minutes
Main cooking utensils: 2 6-inch (15-cm.) sponge sandwich tins
Oven temperature: moderate (375°F., 190°C., Gas Mark 5)
Oven position: about 2 rungs from top of oven
Serves: 6

Imperial
4 oz. margarine or butter
4 oz. castor sugar
2 large eggs
4 oz. self-raising flour (or plain flour and 1 level teaspoon baking powder)
Filling:
3 tablespoons jam
Decoration:
castor or sieved icing sugar

Metric
125 g. margarine or butter
125 g. castor sugar
2 large eggs
125 g. self-raising flour (or plain flour and 1 level teaspoon baking powder)
Filling:
3 tablespoons jam
Decoration:
castor or sieved icing sugar

1. Cream the margarine or butter and sugar until soft and light.
2. Whisk eggs, beat gradually into the butter mixture, if the mixture shows signs of curdling add a little sieved flour.
3. Fold in the sieved flour with a metal spoon, taking care not to overhandle.
4. Put into greased and floured or lined tins.
5. Bake for time and at temperature given.
6. Test cakes before removing from oven. Press gently with finger, if no impression remains the cake is cooked.
7. Cool on a wire cooling tray, sandwich with jam, decorate with castor or icing sugar. In an airtight tin, this cake keeps well for several days.

Note: When baking always check oven temperatures with that recommended in your cooker instruction card or book.

Variations

Coffee sponge: Use 2 small eggs mixed with 1 tablespoon coffee essence.

Chocolate sponge: Use $3\frac{1}{2}$ oz. (110 g.) flour and $\frac{1}{2}$ oz. (15 g.) cocoa.

Sponge cake

Cooking time: 20 minutes
Preparation time: 10–15 minutes
Main cooking utensil: 6- to 7-inch (15- to 18-cm.) cake tin
Oven temperature: moderate (375°F., 190°C., Gas Mark 5)
Oven position: centre
Serves: 5–6

Imperial

2 large eggs
2–3 oz. castor sugar
2 oz. flour (plain can be used with no baking powder or with ½ level teaspoon, or use self-raising flour)
1 dessertspoon hot water
Coating:
little butter
shaking of flour or flour and castor sugar

Metric

2 large eggs
50–75 g. castor sugar
50 g. flour (plain can be used with no baking powder or with ½ level teaspoon, or use self-raising flour)
1 dessertspoon hot water
Coating:
little butter
shaking of flour or flour and castor sugar

1. Put the eggs and sugar into a large mixing bowl, and whisk until the mixture is thick and creamy (you see the trail of the whisk). If done over hot water continue beating until the mixture cools again.
2. Sieve the flour at least once.
3. Fold gently into the egg mixture with a metal spoon. Lastly fold in the water.
4. Grease the tin lightly, then coat with flour or an equal mixture of flour and castor sugar.
5. Spoon the mixture carefully into the tin.
6. Bake for time and at temperature given.
7. Test cake before removing from the oven – press with finger, if no impression remains the cake is cooked.
8. Turn the cake out carefully, allowing it 1 minute to cool in the tin. Split and fill with jam or cream.

Variation

Bake in 2 6-inch (15-cm.) sandwich tins towards top of moderately hot oven (400°F., 200°C., Gas Mark 6) for approximately 8–9 minutes.

Swiss roll

Cooking time: 7–10 minutes
Preparation time: 10–15 minutes
Main cooking utensil: lined Swiss roll tin 9 by 12 inches (23 by 30 cm.), greaseproof paper
Oven temperature: hot (400–450°F., 200–230°C., Gas Mark 6–7)
Oven position: near top
Serves: 8

Imperial	Metric
3 large eggs	3 large eggs
3–4 oz. castor sugar	75–100 g. castor sugar
3 oz. flour (plain can be used with no baking powder or with ½ level teaspoon, or self-raising flour)	75 g. flour (plain can be used with no baking powder or with ½ level teaspoon, or self-raising flour)
1 tablespoon hot water	1 tablespoon hot water
little castor sugar	little castor sugar
Filling:	*Filling:*
4–6 tablespoons warm jam	4–6 tablespoons warm jam
Decoration:	*Decoration:*
castor sugar	castor sugar

1. Put the eggs and sugar into a large mixing bowl, and whisk until the mixture is thick and creamy (you see the trail of the whisk). If done over hot water continue beating until the mixture cools again.
2. Sieve the flour at least once.
3. Fold gently into the egg mixture with a metal spoon. Lastly fold in the water.
4. Pour into the tin, lined with greased greaseproof paper.
5. Bake for time and at temperature given.
6. Test cake before removing from the oven. Press with finger, if no impression remains the cake is cooked.
7. Turn on to sugared paper, spread with jam, roll firmly and dredge with sugar. To serve, cut in slices.

Note: When baking always check oven temperatures with that recommended in your cooker instruction card or book.

Variation

Roll round paper, allow to cool, then fill with whipped cream or cream and jam.

Gugelhupf

Cooking time: 30–40 minutes depending on width of tin
Preparation time: 20 minutes
Main cooking utensil: fluted tin – Gugelhupf mould as illustrated
Oven temperature: moderate (350–375°F., 180–190°C., Gas Mark 4–5)
Oven position: centre
Serves: 8–12

Imperial	Metric
4½ oz. butter	125 g. butter
4½ oz. castor sugar	125 g. castor sugar
grated rind of 1 lemon	grated rind of 1 lemon
4 eggs	4 eggs
4½ oz. plain flour	125 g. plain flour

1. Cream the softened butter, sugar and finely grated lemon rind until very light and fluffy.
2. Separate egg yolks and whites.
3. Gradually beat in the egg yolks.
4. Stir the sieved flour into the mixture.
5. Whisk the egg whites until stiff and fold evenly into the mixture.
6. Fill greased and floured tin three-quarters full.
7. Bake until the cake is golden brown and firm to the touch.
8. Turn out carefully.
9. Dust with icing sugar before serving, if desired.

Note: To grease and flour a cake tin, brush the tin with melted butter, cooking fat or oil. Shake in a little flour and turn tin until it is evenly coated. Shake out any surplus flour.

When baking always check oven temperatures with that recommended in your cooker instruction card or book.

Apfelstrudel

Cooking time: 50 minutes
Preparation time: 45 minutes
Main cooking utensil: baking tray or sheet
Oven temperature: hot (425–450°F., 220–230°C., Gas Mark 7–8), then moderate (350–375°F., 180–190°C., Gas Mark 4–5)
Serves: 6

Imperial

Strudel dough:
8 oz. plain flour
pinch salt
1 egg yolk
1 tablespoon melted butter
about $\frac{1}{4}$ pint warm water

Filling:
1$\frac{1}{2}$ lb. prepared cooking apples
2 oz. currants
2 oz. stoned raisins
2 oz. dry breadcrumbs, fried in butter
2 oz. castor sugar
$\frac{1}{2}$ tablespoon ground cinnamon
grated rind of $\frac{1}{2}$ lemon
4 oz. melted butter

Glaze:
little melted butter

Metric

Strudel dough:
200 g. plain flour
pinch salt
1 egg yolk
1 tablespoon melted butter
about 125 ml. warm water

Filling:
600 g. prepared cooking apples
50 g. currants
50 g. stoned raisins
50 g. dry breadcrumbs, fried in butter
50 g. castor sugar
$\frac{1}{2}$ tablespoon ground cinnamon
grated rind of $\frac{1}{2}$ lemon
100 g. melted butter

Glaze:
little melted butter.

1. Place the flour and salt into a warmed basin.
2. Make a well in the centre and stir in the beaten egg yolk, melted butter and sufficient warm water to make a soft dough.
3. Knead thoroughly on a warmed well-floured board.
4. Cover and stand for 15 minutes.
5. Roll out on a floured cloth – pull and roll dough until paper thin.
6. To make the filling, mix the peeled sliced apples with the rest of the ingredients.
7. When dough is ready, trim off thick edges, spread with apple mixture leaving 1 inch (2$\frac{1}{2}$ cm.) uncovered round edges.
8. Gently roll up with filling inside.
9. Pinch edges together and place on greased baking sheet.
10. Brush top with melted butter. Bake for 20 minutes in centre of hot oven, then 30 minutes at lower temperature. Serve with whipped cream.

Variation

Chocolate strudel: Add 2 oz. (50 g.) chocolate to the flour (see picture).

Streusel torte

Cooking time: about 45 minutes
Preparation time: 20 minutes plus time for proving
Main cooking utensils: saucepan, baking tin with deep sides
Oven temperature: moderate (375°F., 190°C., Gas Mark 5)
Oven position: centre
Serves: 10–12

Imperial	Metric
1 oz. yeast	25 g. yeast
$\frac{1}{4}$ pint milk	125 ml. milk
2 tablespoons sugar	2 tablespoons sugar
1 teaspoon salt	1 teaspoon salt
2 eggs	2 eggs
6 tablespoons melted butter	6 tablespoons melted butter
grated rind of 1 lemon	grated rind of 1 lemon
10 oz. plain flour	250 g. plain flour
Streusel:	*Streusel:*
8 oz. sugar	200 g. sugar
6 oz. butter	150 g. butter
1 tablespoon cinnamon	1 tablespoon cinnamon
2 oz. flour	50 g. flour
3–4 oz. melted butter	75–100 g. melted butter

1. Dissolve yeast in the warm milk.
2. Add sugar and salt. Stir well, allow to stand for 5 minutes in a warm place.
3. Beat eggs well; melt the butter.
4. Add beaten eggs and lemon rind to the yeast mixture.
5. Stir in sieved flour and melted butter, alternately. Beat until well mixed with a wooden spoon.
6. Turn dough on to a floured board and leave in a warm place for 10 minutes, covered with a cloth.
7. Knead well until the dough is smooth.
8. Put into a greased bowl, cover and allow to prove for 45 minutes, until the bulk is doubled.
9. Roll dough out to $\frac{3}{8}$-inch ($\frac{1}{2}$-cm.) thickness. Place in a greased tin. Dust top with flour, leave to prove for a further 40 minutes.
10. Mix ingredients for the streusel together, except the melted butter.
11. When dough has risen, brush top with melted butter.
12. Spread the streusel on top.
13. Bake for time and at temperature given.

Rich chocolate cake

Cooking time: $1\frac{1}{4}$ hours
Preparation time: 40 minutes
Main cooking utensils: 8-inch (20-cm.) cake tin, saucepan
Oven temperature: moderate (350–375°F., 180–190°C., Gas Mark 4–5)
Oven position: centre
Serves: 12–16

Imperial	Metric
8 oz. butter	225 g. butter
8 oz. soft brown sugar	225 g. soft brown sugar
6 oz. black treacle	175 g. black treacle
4 eggs	4 eggs
8 oz. self-raising flour	225 g. self-raising flour
2 oz. cocoa	55 g. cocoa
Orange butter cream:	*Orange butter cream:*
5 oz. butter	150 g. butter
10 oz. sieved icing sugar	275 g. sieved icing sugar
grated rind and juice of 1 orange	grated rind and juice of 1 orange
apricot jam	apricot jam
Chocolate coating:	*Chocolate coating:*
$\frac{1}{4}$ pint evaporated milk	142 ml. evaporated milk
$\frac{1}{2}$ oz. butter	15 g. butter
6 oz. plain chocolate	175 g. plain chocolate
chocolate vermicelli	chocolate vermicelli

1. Cream together butter, sugar and treacle until soft and light.
2. Gradually beat in the eggs, adding a little sieved flour if the mixture shows signs of curdling.
3. Fold in the sieved flour and cocoa.
4. Put into a greased and floured or lined tin and bake for time given.
5. Test to see if cooked by pressing firmly on top, allow to cool.
6. Cream butter and icing sugar with the orange juice and rind, then split the cake into three layers and sandwich with the orange cream.
7. Coat the cake with apricot jam.
8. Heat milk and butter until nearly boiling, remove from the heat, add the broken chocolate, stir until melted.
9. Pour chocolate over the cake, set for a few minutes, then coat sides with vermicelli. This cake keeps well for several days.

Note: In this recipe the more accurate conversions give a better result.

Moist chocolate sandwich

Cooking time: 25 minutes
Preparation time: 15 minutes
Main cooking utensils: 2 7-inch (18-cm.) sponge sandwich tins
Oven temperature: moderate (375°F., 190°C., Gas Mark 5)
Oven position: about 2 rungs from top of oven
Serves: 8–10

Imperial	Metric
4 oz. margarine or cooking fat	110 g. margarine or cooking fat
4 oz. sugar	110 g. sugar
1 level tablespoon golden syrup	1 level tablespoon golden syrup
2 eggs	2 eggs
6 oz. self-raising flour (or plain flour and 1½ level teaspoons baking powder)	175 g. self-raising flour (or plain flour and 1½ level teaspoons baking powder)
1 oz. cocoa	25 g. cocoa
1 tablespoon milk	1 tablespoon milk
Filling:	*Filling:*
2 oz. butter or margarine	50 g. butter or margarine
2 oz. sieved icing sugar	50 g. sieved icing sugar
½ oz. cocoa	15 g. cocoa
Decoration:	*Decoration:*
sieved icing sugar	sieved icing sugar

1. Cream margarine or cooking fat, sugar and syrup until soft.
2. Whisk eggs, beat gradually into the fat mixture. If the mixture shows signs of curdling add a little sieved flour.
3. Sieve the flour or flour and baking powder with the cocoa and fold in gently with a metal spoon. Add the milk.
4. Put into greased and floured or lined tins.
5. Bake for time and at temperature given.
6. Test cakes before removing from oven. Press gently with finger, if no impression remains cake is cooked.
7. Cool on wire cooling tray then sandwich with chocolate butter icing. Cream the butter and sugar until soft, then add cocoa. Sprinkle the top with sugar.

Note: In this recipe the more exact conversion gives a better result.

Variation
Mocha cake: Use 1 tablespoon coffee instead of milk.

Devil's food cake

Cooking time: 25 minutes
Preparation time: 35 minutes
Main cooking utensils: 2 9-inch (23-cm.) sponge tins
Oven temperature: moderate (375°F., 190°C., Gas Mark 5)
Oven position: just above centre
Serves: 8-10

Imperial	Metric
2 oz. butter	50 g. butter
8 oz. sugar	200 g. sugar
2 eggs	2 eggs
6 oz. self-raising flour	150 g. self-raising flour
4 tablespoons sour milk	4 tablespoons sour milk
6 tablespoons boiling black coffee	6 tablespoons boiling black coffee
2 oz. plain melted chocolate	50 g. plain melted chocolate
1 level teaspoon bicarbonate of soda	1 level teaspoon bicarbonate of soda
1 teaspoon vanilla essence	1 teaspoon vanilla essence
Frosting:	*Frosting:*
1 egg white	1 egg white
3 dessertspoons cold water	3 dessertspoons cold water
7 oz. granulated sugar	175 g. granulated sugar
$\frac{1}{4}$ teaspoon cream of tartar	$\frac{1}{4}$ teaspoon cream of tartar
$\frac{1}{2}$ teaspoon vanilla essence	$\frac{1}{2}$ teaspoon vanilla essence
little melted chocolate	little melted chocolate

1. Cream the butter and sugar, beat until light.
2. Beat in the eggs a little at a time.
3. Add a little flour and sour milk alternately and end by adding flour.
4. Pour boiling coffee on to the melted chocolate and add bicarbonate of soda.
5. Cool slightly and add to the mixture.
6. Stir in the vanilla essence, and put into prepared tins.
7. Bake for time and at temperature given.
8. When cool fill and spread with icing.
9. To make the frosting, whisk all the ingredients except vanilla in the basin over boiling water for 7 minutes until mixture stands in peaks; add the vanilla essence.
10. Decorate with a little melted chocolate in a ribbon design as shown in the picture.

Variation

A little spice may be added to the flour.

Strawberry shortcake

Cooking time: 20 minutes
Preparation time: 20 minutes
Main cooking utensils: 2 7-inch (18-cm.) lined sandwich tins
Oven temperature: moderately hot (375–400°F., 190–200°C., Gas Mark 5–6)
Oven position: second rung from top
Serves: 6–8

Imperial	Metric
4 oz. margarine	100 g. margarine
4 oz. castor sugar	100 g. castor sugar
4 oz. self-raising flour (or plain flour with 1 level teaspoon baking powder)	100 g. self-raising flour (or plain flour with 1 level teaspoon baking powder)
2 oz. cornflour	50 g. cornflour
2 eggs	2 eggs
Filling and topping:	*Filling and topping:*
1 small punnet fresh strawberries	1 small punnet fresh strawberries
$\frac{1}{4}$ pint thick cream	142 ml. thick cream
1 egg white	1 egg white
sugar to taste	sugar to taste

1. Cream margarine and sugar until light and soft.
2. Sieve the flour (or flour and baking powder) and cornflour.
3. Add beaten eggs to creamed margarine, then fold in the flour with a metal spoon.
4. Place the mixture in the tins, and flatten the top.
5. Bake for time and at temperature given until crisp and golden.
6. Cool on wire cooling tray.
7. Prepare strawberries; whip cream in one bowl and egg white in another, fold together and sweeten if wished.
8. Cover one shortcake with some of the strawberries and cream.
9. Top with second shortcake and rest of cream and fruit. Serve sliced.

Note: This cake keeps before decorating for 1–2 days only. When baking always check oven temperatures with that recommended in your cooker instruction card or book.

Variation
Use other dessert fruit, e.g., mix dessert pears with strawberries.

Coffee carnival gâteau

Cooking time: 20 minutes
Preparation time: 35 minutes
Main cooking utensils: 2 7-inch (18-cm.) sandwich tins
Oven temperature: moderate (375°F., 190°C., Gas Mark 5)
Oven position: just above centre
Serves: 8

Imperial

4 oz. butter
4 oz. sugar
2 eggs
4 oz. self-raising flour (or with plain flour use 1 level teaspoon baking powder)

Coffee butter icing:

6 oz. butter
9 oz. sieved icing sugar
2 tablespoons coffee essence
2 oz. flaked almonds, lightly browned

Metric

125 g. butter
125 g. sugar
2 eggs
125 g. self-raising flour (or with plain flour use 1 level teaspoon baking powder)

Coffee butter icing:

175 g. butter
250 g. sieved icing sugar
2 tablespoons coffee essence
50 g. flaked almonds, lightly browned

1. Cream together butter and sugar until light and fluffy.
2. Gradually beat in the eggs.
3. Fold in the sieved flour and put into the greased or greased and lined tins.
4. Bake until firm, then turn out on to a wire cooling tray to cool.
5. To make the icing, cream the butter then add sieved icing sugar and continue creaming until light.
6. Gradually beat in coffee essence.
7. Split each sandwich and fill with the butter icing.
8. Spread the remaining coffee butter icing over the top and sides of the cake.
9. Press browned almonds all over the top and sides.

Note: To blanch almonds to flake or chop, put in boiling water for 1 minute, remove skins, dry.

When baking always check oven temperatures with that recommended in your cooker instruction card or book.

Variation

Mocha gâteau: Use 3½ oz. (110 g.) flour and ½ oz. (15 g.) cocoa.

Chocolate bar gâteau

Cooking time: 20 minutes
Preparation time: 40 minutes
Main cooking utensils: 2 7-inch (18-cm.) sponge tins
Oven temperature: moderate (375°F., 190°C., Gas Mark 5)
Oven position: just above centre
Serves: 8–10

Imperial	Metric
4 oz. margarine	100 g. margarine
4 oz. castor sugar	100 g. castor sugar
2 eggs	2 eggs
6 oz. self-raising flour	150 g. self-raising flour
Decoration:	*Decoration:*
6 oz. sieved icing sugar	150 g. sieved icing sugar
3 oz. butter or margarine	75 g. butter or margarine
2 teaspoons cold water	2 teaspoons cold water
chocolate vermicelli or grated chocolate	chocolate vermicelli or grated chocolate
5 small bars chocolate	5 small bars chocolate

1. Cream the margarine and sugar together until light and fluffy.
2. Gradually beat in the whisked eggs.
3. Fold in the sieved flour adding sufficient warm water to form a soft dropping consistency.
4. Turn into 2 greased and floured sponge tins.
5. Bake for time and at temperature given.
6. Make the butter cream by creaming together the icing sugar and butter. Add enough water to form a piping consistency.
7. Use part of this to sandwich together the two sponges.
8. Spread a thin layer around the edge of the sponge and roll in the chocolate vermicelli. Cover the top with icing.
9. Cut each chocolate bar very carefully into half to give diagonal pieces.
10. Press on to the butter icing.
11. Decorate with rosettes of butter icing.

Note: To roll cakes in either chopped nuts or vermicelli, put this on greaseproof paper and roll out cake like a hoop.

West Indian gâteau

Cooking time: 30 minutes
Preparation time: 35 minutes
Main cooking utensils: 2 7-inch (18-cm.) lined tins
Oven temperature: moderate (375°F., 190°C., Gas Mark 5)
Oven position: above centre
Serves: 10–12

Imperial	Metric
6 oz. butter or margarine	150 g. butter or margarine
6 oz. castor sugar	150 g. castor sugar
6 level tablespoons black treacle	6 level tablespoons black treacle
3 eggs	3 eggs
2 oz. cornflour	50 g. cornflour
6 oz. self-raising flour	150 g. self-raising flour
3 tablespoons milk	3 tablespoons milk
Rum butter cream:	*Rum butter cream:*
8 oz. butter	200 g. butter
12 oz. sieved icing sugar	300 g. sieved icing sugar
2 level tablespoons black treacle	2 level tablespoons black treacle
2 tablespoons rum	2 tablespoons rum
4 tablespoons milk	4 tablespoons milk
4 tablespoons hot water	4 tablespoons hot water

1. Cream the butter or margarine, sugar and treacle together until soft and light.
2. Gradually beat in the eggs, adding a little sieved flour if the mixture shows signs of curdling.
3. Fold in the sieved cornflour, flour and milk.
4. Put into lined tins and bake for time given; test to see if cooked by pressing firmly on top. Allow to cool.
5. To make the butter cream, beat butter, icing sugar and treacle well together; gradually beat in the rum, milk and finally the water.
6. Cut each cake in half and sandwich with some of the rum butter cream.
7. Coat the cake with the rest of the mixture and decorate with a ridged design made by pulling a small knife across the icing.

Variation

Use 1 oz. (25 g.) cornflour and 1 oz. (25 g.) cocoa instead of 2 oz. (50 g.) cornflour.

Marshmallow gâteau

Cooking time: 20–25 minutes
Preparation time: 35 minutes
Main cooking utensils: 2 7- to 8-inch (18- to 20-cm.) sandwich tins, saucepan
Oven temperature: moderate (375°F., 190°C., Gas Mark 5)
Oven position: above centre
Serves: 10–12

Imperial	**Metric**
6 oz. margarine or butter	150 g. margarine or butter
6 oz. castor sugar	150 g. castor sugar
3 eggs	3 eggs
6 oz. sieved self-raising flour (or plain flour and $1\frac{1}{2}$ level teaspoons baking powder)	150 g. sieved self-raising flour (or plain flour and $1\frac{1}{2}$ level teaspoons baking powder)
Filling and icing:	*Filling and icing:*
6 oz. marshmallows	150 g. marshmallows
3 tablespoons milk	3 tablespoons milk
3 egg whites	3 egg whites
$1\frac{1}{2}$ oz. castor sugar	40 g. castor sugar

1. Cream together margarine or butter and sugar until light and fluffy.
2. Gradually beat in eggs, adding a little flour if the mixture shows signs of curdling.
3. Fold in flour with a metal spoon.
4. Bake in prepared tins for time and at temperature given.
5. To make the filling, melt the marshmallows slowly in the warmed milk, allow to cool, stirring occasionally.
6. Whisk egg whites until stiff, beat in the sugar gradually, whisk slowly on to marshmallow mixture. Leave until thickened.
7. Sandwich together the cooled cakes with some of the marshmallow and cover top and sides with remainder, swirling up in peaks with a knife.

Variation

Chocolate sponge: Use 5 oz. (125 g.) flour, 1 oz. (25 g.) cocoa.

Lemon sponge: Add the grated rind of 1–2 lemons and a little lemon juice.

Coffee sponge: Add 1 tablespoon coffee essence and use medium eggs.

Cherry and almond cake

Cooking time: 1 hour
Preparation time: 30 minutes
Main cooking utensils: 7-inch (18-cm.) cake tin, greaseproof paper
Oven temperature: slow (300–325°F., 150–170°C., Gas Mark 2–3)
Serves: 8

Imperial	Metric
4 oz. butter or margarine	100 g. butter or margarine
3 oz. soft brown sugar	75 g. soft brown sugar
1 tablespoon black treacle	1 tablespoon black treacle
2 eggs	2 eggs
6 oz. self-raising flour	150 g. self-raising flour
½ teaspoon mixed spice	½ teaspoon mixed spice
2 oz. sultanas or seeded raisins	50 g. sultanas or seeded raisins
3 tablespoons milk	3 tablespoons milk
Topping:	*Topping:*
4 tablespoons warmed sieved apricot jam	4 tablespoons warmed sieved apricot jam
2 oz. flaked brown almonds	50 g. flaked browned almonds
4 oz. Maraschino or glacé cherries	100 g. Maraschino or glacé cherries

1. Cream butter or margarine, sugar and treacle together until soft and light.
2. Beat the eggs, add to the mixture slowly, so that it remains stiff.
3. Fold in the sieved flour and mixed spice, sultanas and finally the milk.
4. Turn into the greased and lined cake tin.
5. Bake in the centre of the oven for time and at temperature given.
6. Allow to cool slightly in the tin before turning it on to a wire cooling tray.
7. To decorate, spread the side of the cake with a little apricot jam.
8. Roll carefully in the nuts. Arrange halved cherries on top of the cake and brush these with the warmed jam glaze.

Note: To brown almonds, either brown on a baking tray in the oven or under the grill turning over as necessary, or fry in hot butter and drain.

Honey almond dessert cake

Cooking time: 45 minutes
Preparation time: 30 minutes
Main cooking utensil: lined 7-inch (18-cm.) cake tin
Oven temperature: moderate (350–375°F., 180–190°C., Gas Mark 4–5)
Oven position: centre
Serves: 6–8

Imperial
4 oz. butter or margarine
2 oz. moist brown sugar
2 level tablespoons thick honey
2 medium-sized eggs
6 oz. self-raising flour
4 tablespoons milk
Topping and filling:
3 oz. butter
$1\frac{1}{2}$ level tablespoons thick honey
3 oz. sieved icing sugar
$1\frac{1}{2}$ oz. flaked toasted almonds
(see page 111)

Metric
100 g. butter or margarine
50 g. moist brown sugar
2 level tablespoons thick honey
2 medium-sized eggs
150 g. self-raising flour
4 tablespoons milk
Topping and filling:
75 g. butter
$1\frac{1}{2}$ level tablespoons thick honey
75 g. sieved icing sugar
40 g. flaked toasted almonds
(see page 111)

1. Cream butter or margarine, sugar and honey together until soft and light.
2. Gradually beat in the eggs, adding a little sieved flour if the mixture shows signs of curdling.
3. Fold in sieved flour and milk.
4. Bake for time and at temperature given.
5. Allow to cool, then split through the centre, fill with part of the honey butter cream.
6. To make this, cream butter well, add the honey and sugar.
7. Spread the remaining mixture over the top and sides of the cake, then press the almonds on top.

Note: When baking always check oven temperatures with that recommended in your cooker instruction card or book.

Variation
A lighter coloured cake is made with castor sugar instead of the brown.

Festive cream gâteau

Cooking time: 30 minutes
Preparation time: 35 minutes
Main cooking utensils: 12- by 8-inch (30- by 20-cm.) Swiss roll tin, greaseproof paper
Oven temperature: moderate (375°F., 190°C., Gas Mark 5)
Oven position: just above centre
Serves: 10–12

Imperial

6 oz. butter or margarine
6 oz. castor sugar
2–3 drops vanilla essence
3 eggs
6 oz. self-raising flour
2 tablespoons hot water

Filling and topping:

$\frac{1}{2}$ pint double cream
4 tablespoons rose hip syrup

Decoration:

5–6 tablespoons lightly toasted desiccated coconut
few segments mandarin orange
a few halved walnuts

Metric

150 g. butter or margarine
150 g. castor sugar
2–3 drops vanilla essence
3 eggs
150 g. self-raising flour
2 tablespoons hot water

Filling and topping:

250 ml. double cream
4 tablespoons rose hip syrup

Decoration:

5–6 tablespoons lightly toasted desiccated coconut
few segments mandarin orange
a few halved walnuts

1. Cream the butter or margarine and sugar until soft and light, adding the essence.
2. Gradually beat in the eggs, adding a little sieved flour if the mixture shows signs of curdling.
3. Fold in the flour and hot water.
4. Line the tin with greaseproof paper, make sure this stands above the top of the tin to support the cake.
5. Bake for time and at temperature given until firm to the touch.
6. Cool, cut into 3 strips.
7. Whip the cream lightly, then gradually add the rose hip syrup, taking care not to overbeat.
8. Sandwich the layers together with some of the rose hip cream.
9. Coat sides of the cake with the cream and roll in the coconut.
10. Top with cream, mandarin orange segments and walnuts and pipe rosettes of cream on top if wished. Serve as a special cake for tea or instead of a sweet. This is an ideal choice at Christmas time to make a change from the rich fruity cake and pudding mixtures.

Mother's day cake

Cooking time: 20 minutes
Preparation time: 40 minutes
Main cooking utensils: 2 7-inch (18-cm.) sandwich tins, basin, No. 1 or 2 writing pipe, icing syringe or greaseproof paper bag
Oven temperature: moderate (375°F., 190°C., Gas Mark 5)
Oven position: second rung from top
Serves: 8–10

Imperial	**Metric**
4 oz. margarine	125 g. margarine
4 oz. castor sugar	125 g. castor sugar
grated rind of 1 lemon	grated rind of 1 lemon
2 eggs	2 eggs
4 oz. self-raising flour	125 g. self-raising flour
Lemon icing:	*Lemon icing:*
4 oz. margarine	125 g. margarine
12 oz. sieved icing sugar	350 g. sieved icing sugar
good 2 tablespoons lemon juice	good 2 tablespoons lemon juice
Decoration:	*Decoration:*
yellow colouring	yellow colouring
cake board	cake board
1 rose spray	1 rose spray
band ribbon	band ribbon

1. Cream the margarine and sugar until soft and light, with the lemon rind.
2. Gradually beat in the eggs, adding a little sieved flour if the mixture shows signs of curdling.
3. Fold in the rest of the flour; if the eggs are small add 1 dessertspoon water (lemon juice could be used).
4. Put into the greased and floured tins and bake for time and at temperature given, until firm to the touch.
5. Turn out and allow to cool.
6. To make the icing, cream the margarine and half the sugar until soft, add the remaining icing sugar with the lemon juice, beat again. Save some for piping.
7. Use a little icing to sandwich the cakes together, put the remainder into a basin over a pan of hot water, beat until smooth, glossy and soft.
8. Pour over the cake and allow to set.
9. Tint the small amount of icing left a deeper colour and pipe the word MOTHER. Lift on to a cake board, put rose and ribbon in position.

Simnel cake

Cooking time: $2\frac{1}{4}$ hours
Preparation time: 40 minutes
Main cooking utensil: 8-inch (20-cm.) cake tin
Oven temperature: moderate (325–350°F., 170–180°C., Gas Mark 3–4) reducing slightly if necessary
Serves: 10–12

Imperial	Metric
6 oz. margarine	175 g. margarine
6 oz. castor sugar	175 g. castor sugar
3 eggs	3 eggs
8 oz. plain flour	225 g. plain flour
1 teaspoon baking powder	1 teaspoon baking powder
1 teaspoon mixed spice	1 teaspoon mixed spice
1 lb. mixed dried fruit	450 g. mixed dried fruit
3 oz. chopped glacé cherries	75 g. chopped glacé cherries
3 oz. chopped candied peel	75 g. chopped candied peel
2 oz. chopped blanched almonds (optional)	50 g. chopped blanched almonds (optional)
2 tablespoons milk	2 tablespoons milk
Marzipan:	*Marzipan:*
8 oz. ground almonds	225 g. ground almonds
4 oz. castor sugar	100 g. castor sugar
4 oz. sieved icing sugar	100 g. sieved icing sugar
2 egg yolks or 1 egg to bind	2 egg yolks or 1 egg to bind
Glaze:	*Glaze:*
egg white	egg white

1. Cream the margarine and sugar until soft and light. Gradually beat in the eggs, add a little sieved flour if mixture shows signs of curdling.
2. Sieve the flour, baking powder, and spice, fold into the egg mixture, add fruit and milk.
3. Make the marzipan by mixing the ingredients together, roll out just under half to 8-inch (20-cm.) round.
4. Put half cake mixture into greased and floured cake tin, cover with marzipan and then the rest of the cake.
5. Bake in the centre of the oven for time and at temperature given.
6. Test to see if cooked by pressing firmly and listening. If cooked the cake is silent, if uncooked there is a distinct humming noise.
7. Allow the cake to cool on a wire tray.
8. Roll out the rest of the marzipan, cover the top and make small Easter eggs (colouring these if wished) with marzipan.
9. Brush top with egg white and brown for a little time under a low grill.
10. Decorate with chickens, etc.

Coffee frosted brownies

Cooking time: 25–30 minutes
Preparation time: 20 minutes
Main cooking utensil: 7- by 11-inch (18- by 27-cm.) Swiss roll tin
Oven temperature: moderate (325–350°F., 170–180°C., Gas Mark 3–4)
Makes: 21 brownies

Imperial	Metric
3 oz. plain flour	75 g. plain flour
$1\frac{1}{2}$ oz. cocoa powder	40 g. cocoa powder
$\frac{1}{2}$ level teaspoon baking powder	$\frac{1}{2}$ level teaspoon baking powder
4 oz. butter or margarine	100 g. butter or margarine
8 oz. soft brown sugar	200 g. soft brown sugar
1 teaspoon vanilla essence	1 teaspoon vanilla essence
2 large eggs	2 large eggs
Coffee frosting:	*Coffee frosting:*
2 oz. butter	50 g. butter
2 tablespoons coffee essence	2 tablespoons coffee essence
8 oz. sieved icing sugar	200 g. sieved icing sugar
1 tablespoon milk	1 tablespoon milk
Decoration:	*Decoration:*
2 oz. walnut halves	50 g. walnut halves

1. Sieve together flour, cocoa and baking powder.
2. Cream butter or margarine, sugar and vanilla essence until light and fluffy.
3. Beat in the eggs, one at a time.
4. Stir in the dry ingredients.
5. Put the mixture into a greased tin.
6. Bake just above centre of oven, for time and at temperature given, until firm to touch. Cut into 21 fingers while still warm, remove from tin and cool on a wire rack.
7. Melt the butter in a pan; add coffee essence; bring slowly to boil, then boil steadily for 2 minutes.
8. Combine quickly with the icing sugar, pour in the milk then beat until frosting is cold and stiff enough to spread.
9. Cover tops of brownies with frosting then decorate each with a walnut half.

Variation

Add 2 oz. (50 g.) chopped chocolate to the cake mixture before baking.

Ginger prune crunch

Preparation time: 15 minutes
Utensil for setting: 7-inch (18-cm.) square cake tin or sandwich tin
Serves: 8

Imperial	Metric
8 oz. ginger biscuits	200 g. ginger biscuits
4 oz. stoned uncooked prunes	100 g. stoned uncooked prunes
1 oz. walnuts	25 g. walnuts
2 oz. butter	50 g. butter
2 tablespoons golden syrup	2 tablespoons golden syrup
Decoration:	*Decoration:*
castor sugar	castor sugar

1. Crush the ginger biscuits until they are crumbs and small pieces. Do not make too even in texture.
2. Chop the prunes, remove the stones, add chopped walnuts.
3. Melt the butter with the syrup.
4. Pour on to the dry ingredients.
5. Stir together to form a firm mixture and press out in the tin.
6. Leave to become quite cold and firm. Chill if preferred, but do not allow to become too cold.
7. Cut into fingers. Serve sprinkled with castor sugar. Could be served with cooked fruit for a sweet.

Note: You can sometimes buy stoned prunes, which would be good for this recipe.

Variation
Use half chopped figs and half chopped prunes, or all figs, or all dried apricots.

Chocolate and walnut cookies

Cooking time: 10–12 minutes
Preparation time: 20 minutes
Main cooking utensils: baking trays or sheets
Oven temperature: moderate (375°F., 190°C., Gas Mark 5)
Oven position: centre
Makes: 40–50

Imperial

6 oz. self-raising flour or 6 oz. plain flour and 1½ teaspoons baking powder
3 oz. butter
3 oz. brown sugar
3 oz. granulated sugar
½ teaspoon vanilla essence
½ teaspoon water
1 egg
2 oz. chopped walnuts
4 oz. (1 packet) Chocolate Polka Dots (chocolate chips)

Metric

150 g. self-raising flour or 150 g. plain flour and 1½ teaspoons baking powder
75 g. butter
75 g. brown sugar
75 g. granulated sugar
½ teaspoon vanilla essence
½ teaspoon water
1 egg
50 g. chopped walnuts
100 g. Chocolate Polka Dots (chocolate chips)

1. Sieve the self-raising flour or plain flour and 1½ teaspoons baking powder.
2. Cream butter, both lots of sugar, vanilla and water until soft and light.
3. Gradually beat in the egg and then flour.
4. Add nuts and Chocolate Polka Dots; the mixture should be quite soft.
5. Drop teaspoons of the mixture on to greased trays, allowing room to spread.
6. Bake for time and at temperature given until crisp and golden brown. Serve with tea, coffee or with a plain sweet.

Note: As this makes a lot of small biscuits you may have to hold back some trays as they must not be baked in the hotter parts of the oven.

Variation

Omit nuts and put in sultanas.

Brandy snaps

Cooking time: 5–6 minutes
Preparation time: 15 minutes
Main cooking utensils: saucepan, well-greased baking trays or sheets
Oven temperature: moderate (375°F., 190°C., Gas Mark 5)
Oven position: just above centre
Makes: 18 snaps

Imperial	Metric
2 oz. butter	50 g. butter
2 oz. castor sugar	50 g. castor sugar
2 oz. black treacle	50 g. black treacle
1 teaspoon lemon juice	1 teaspoon lemon juice
scant 2 oz. plain flour	scant 50 g. plain flour
$\frac{1}{2}$–1 level teaspoon ground ginger	$\frac{1}{2}$–1 level teaspoon ground ginger

1. Melt butter, sugar, black treacle and lemon juice together over gentle heat.
2. Add sieved flour and ginger, blend together.
3. Put teaspoonfuls of the mixture on well-greased trays, 5 inches (13 cm.) apart.
4. Bake for approximately 5 minutes until a rich brown and well spread out. Only put one tray in the oven at a time so you can roll without difficulty.
5. Remove from oven, leave to cool for 1 minute until they are easily lifted.
6. While still warm wrap each one round a wooden handle, working quickly. Allow to become firm before lifting on to a wire tray. To serve, fill with fresh whipped cream.

Note: Store brandy snaps in an airtight tin.

Variation

Use golden syrup instead of treacle.

Acknowledgements

The following photographs are by courtesy of:

Cadbury Schweppes Foods Limited: pages 22, 90, 98, 104
Flour Advisory Bureau: page 10
Fruit Producers' Council: pages 16, 32, 52, 56, 58, 72
Gale's Honey: pages 46, 64
Lard Information Bureau: pages 12, 38
Lyons Coffee: page 88
P.R. Associates: page 100
RHM Foods Limited: pages 48, 62